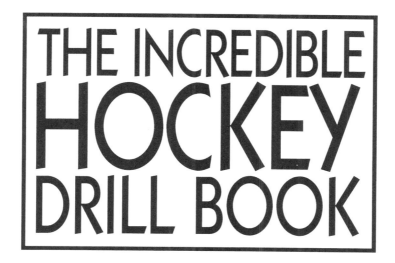

THE INCREDIBLE HOCKEY DRILL BOOK

THE INCREDIBLE HOCKEY DRILL BOOK

•MORE THAN 600 DRILLS•

DAVE CHAMBERS

CONTEMPORARY
BOOKS
A TRIBUNE NEW MEDIA COMPANY

Library of Congress Cataloging-in-Publication Data

Chambers, Dave, 1940–
    The incredible hockey drill book : more than 600 drills / Dave
Chambers.
        p.   cm.
    Originally published: Toronto : Key Porter Books, c1994.
    Includes bibliographical references (p. 151).
    ISBN 0-8092-3254-5 (alk. paper)
    1. Hockey—Coaching.   Hockey—Training.   I. Title.
GV848.25.C44   1995
796.962′07—dc20   95-30788
                                                                CIP

Published by Contemporary Books, Inc.
Two Prudential Plaza, Chicago, Illinois 60601-6790
Manufactured in the United States of America
International Standard Book Number: 0-8092-3254-5

10   9   8   7   6   5   4   3   2   1

Contents

Acknowledgements

I would like to thank all the coaches I have been associated with over the years in both North America and Europe. Many coaches create and collect drills. The ones in this book come from my thirty years of coaching experience and from coaches I have worked with or for, or observed or read about.

I would especially like to thank Robert Thom and Wayne Major of *Hockey Coaching Journal* for the countless hours they spent preparing the diagrams and descriptions of the drills included in this book.

Preface

This book has three parts: the first deals with learning and teaching principles; the second is a collection of inspirational slogans; and the third consists of the drills.

The chapters in Part 1 are intended to assist coaches in organizing practice sessions and putting together drills so that they build on one another in an effective teaching progression. Less experienced coaches should read these chapters before using the drills. More experienced coaches may also want to refer to these chapters as a way of evaluating the effectiveness of their practice sessions.

Coaches, in my experience, are always looking for words and phrases that will get their team focused and motivated. Slogans for the week, day, or a specific game can be a useful tool. The slogans in Part 2 are drawn from both inside and outside the sporting world. The coach can select whatever suits his or her team.

The drills in Part 3 are generally listed in order from simple to complex. It is up to the coach to decide which drills are appropriate for the age and skill level of a particular team or group of players. Properly run practices in which well-executed drills are backed up with good teaching and feedback are the mainstay of effective coaching.

Legend

F Forward	**G** Goaltender	**LW** Left Wing	**LW** Opposition Left Wing
D Defence	**D** Opposition Defence	**RW** Right Wing	**RW** Opposition Right Wing
X Player	**X** Opposition Player	**LD** Left Defence	**BC** Backchecker
C Center	**C** Opposition Center	**RD** Right Defence	**C** Coach
Puck(s)	Bodycheck	Pass	Crossovers
Pylon(s)	Tight/180° turn	Drop Pass	Cariokas
Shot	360° turn	Forward Skating	Backward Skating
— OR | Knee Drop	Pivot		
Screen/Pick	= OR || Stop	Forward Stickhandling	Backward Stickhandling

Part 1
Teaching and Implementing Drills

1

Learning, Teaching, and Analyzing Skills

THE LEARNING PROCESS

The common saying "I hear, I see, I do" is the simplest way of describing how people learn. Coaches apply it by explaining, demonstrating, and practicing a skill. Generally, athletes learn skills by gathering information about a skill, making decisions on how to perform the skill, practicing the skill, and evaluating the result or being provided with feedback on how the skill was performed.

In the learning process, the coach must first assess each player's level of skill. Factors such as age, strength, maturity, and motivation all influence the learning capability of the athlete. If the skills you teach are too easy, your athletes may become bored; and if the skills are too difficult, the athletes may become frustrated with a lack of success.

Feedback
Feedback is an essential part of the learning process. Athletes need to know how well they are performing the skills – and immediate feedback is generally better than delayed feedback. Beginners respond best to visual feedback, while verbal feedback can sometimes be effective with older experienced athletes. In the development of skills, make the feedback specific but give it in limited amounts at one time. It is important that the athlete understand the feedback you are giving.

Whole vs. Part
A complex skill can be learned more easily when it's broken down into separate parts, but the skill should be seen in its entirety first. To make learning effective, each part should be related to the whole skill. An example of the part method would be in the teaching of the hip check where the skill is broken down and practiced as the following elements: backward skating and crouch, hip and body rotation, contact, and knee extension and upward thrust.

When the skill requires coordination of timing and speed, the whole method should be used, i.e. the skill is practiced with all the parts together and in sequence. Generally, it is better to practice a skill as a whole.

Chaining

Chaining refers to learning and connecting the parts that make up a complex skill. When the athlete is learning a skill, he/she learns to link the various distinct parts of the skill. Forward chaining refers to learning a skill by starting with the beginning segment; backward chaining starts at the segment at the end of the skill and works backward. The links are then joined together and the skill is practiced as a whole. An example of forward chaining in the teaching of the slap shot would be starting with the preparation stage, that is, the back swing and moving through the forward swing, impact and follow-through stages. An example of backward chaining would be starting with the follow-through and moving back through the sequence.

Shaping

Shaping is a learning method where the learning of the skill takes place gradually. The skill is briefly demonstrated and then simplified to include only the most important parts. The missing parts are added gradually until the whole skill is learned. Shaping differs from chaining in that the learner may start with any link in the chain, rather than with the beginning or end.

Mental Practice (Imagery)

It has been shown that the mental rehearsal of a skill aids the learning process. Use mental practice in conjunction with physical practice, just before a skill is to be executed, and at times away from the practice situation. The athlete needs some knowledge of the skill before mental practice can be effective.

Mass vs. Distributed Practice

The total number of trials or total time for quality practice is more important than whether practice is massed or distributed. Practice of a skill that is distributed over a number of training sessions is believed to be superior to practicing the skill massed at one training session. Distributed practice is more effective when the skill to be learned is complex or takes a great deal of physical effort or when the athlete is young or just beginning. Massed practice, in some situations, can be successful when used with the highly skilled or mature athletes.

Grouping

Athletes of similar skill levels tend to learn faster when grouped together. Lower skilled athletes tend to learn faster in a mixed-skill group while superior athletes prefer to work with, and learn faster while practicing with, the highly skilled.

Environment

A pleasant, clean, well-lit, positive practice environment enhances learning. Positive, well-planned instruction with proper teaching aids and equipment support the learning process.

Short-Term Memory

Usually an athlete can handle and understand only three or four key teaching points at one time and this information stays with the learner between 20 and 30 seconds. Therefore, it is essential for the athlete to practice the skill being taught immediately after the teaching presentation.

THE TEACHING PROCESS

Select the Skill

The first step in the teaching process is to select the skill or skills to be taught. Factors such as the athletes' present skill level, age, physical maturity, and motivation are important in deciding on the skill progression.

The skills taught should not be too easy or too difficult for the athlete. The progression should always be from simple to complex, and you should have a plan for the progression. As much as possible, skills and drills should be game-like and challenging for the athlete.

Once you've selected the skill, the keys to effective teaching are the explanation, demonstration, practice, feedback, and correction.

Explanation

The explanation should be well-planned. Start the explanation with the importance of the skill. Choose three to five key teaching points with short descriptive phrases. The explanation should not take more than one to one and a half minutes. Remember, learners have short attention spans and start forgetting as soon as 30 seconds after an explanation. Speak clearly and concisely and use direct eye contact with the athletes.

Demonstration

The demonstration in most cases coincides with the explanation of the skill. You must decide what angle the skill is to be viewed from and who demonstrates. If an explanation accompanies the demonstration, it may be advantageous to have a highly skilled athlete demonstrate the skill. If you yourself do not possess the skill, have the skill demonstrated by an athlete or an assistant coach. Some coaches demonstrate skills in slow motion (such as the slap shot) when they do not possess an advanced level of the skill themselves.

Set up the teaching formations so that all the athletes have a good view of you and/or the demonstrator of the skill. No athlete should be behind you when you are talking. Formations such as the semi-circle and U-formation are best. You must also make sure that the athletes are viewing the demonstration from the correct angle as well. End the demonstration as the explanation began, with a review of the key teaching points. Include time for questions or clearing up misunderstandings. Take a maximum of three minutes for the explanation and demonstration.

Practice

Practice the skill immediately after the skill or drill has been explained and demonstrated. Remember, athletes start forgetting shortly after they have had something explained to them. The practice formation or drill should take into account whether the athletes work alone, in pairs, or in groups. Practice drills can be simple or complex, depending on the level and skill of the athlete. The specific aspects of drills will be discussed later.

Feedback

Give feedback and correction during the practice of the skills. Feedback should be specific to individuals and should occur as the skill is being practiced. Give group corrections on common errors.

ANALYSIS OF SKILLS

Giving feedback and analyzing skills can be learned and improved on. Knowing what to observe and how to observe requires knowledge, experience, and practice.

To be able to give feedback, you must understand the key phases of a skill. By observing or using videos of a skilled athlete, you can understand what a properly executed skill should look like. Break the skill down into the important phases and understand the key words for correction (e.g., straighten the stride leg in skating – hip, knee, ankle).

Observing

Make sure you're in the correct position on the ice to observe and be sure to circulate, along with assistant coaches, in order to give feedback to as many athletes as possible.

Once again, your feedback should be specific and be given as soon after the skill is practiced as possible. Observing skills and giving feedback to athletes is a skill *you* must practice and work on. Understanding and picking out common errors is an essential skill for good coaching.

Positive and Negative Feedback

As a general rule, use positive reinforcement approximately 90% of the time. If you want a movement or behavior to be repeated, positively reinforce it. If you do not want a movement or behavior repeated, don't reinforce it or reinforce only the positive aspects of the movement. Negative reinforcement can be used to prevent a movement or behavior being repeated but don't use it on a regular basis. Athletes learn more, and more quickly, in a positive environment.

2
Development of Skills

"How you practice is how you play."

"Perfect practice makes perfect."

"The game is an opportunity to see the results of your teaching."

These quotes have been around for many years in the sporting world, but they still say a great deal about the development of an athlete. The development of individual skills, tactics, strategy, mental preparation, and conditioning are all related to the practice situation. Running effective drills and practices is one of the most important aspects of coaching. Planning the season; the monthly, weekly, and daily practices; and the effective use and progression of drills are all intricate parts of the coaching responsibility. Game day, as many coaches comment, is only the result of all the hard work, preparation, and dedication of athletes and coaches.

PLANNING THE YEAR

You should have a master plan for the entire year. The general areas of planning include the preparation, competitive, and transition periods used throughout the year.

The preparation period (off season) includes a general physical training period and a hockey-specific training period. Each period lasts approximately six to eight weeks.

The competition period is divided into pre-competition (training camp and exhibition), main competition (league schedule), tapering, and playoff competition periods. The pre-competition period includes the training camp and exhibition schedules; the main competition period includes the regularly scheduled games. A tapering or unloading period lasts for a week to 10 days before the playoff competition period begins.

The transition period occurs after the season and playoffs are completed. It involves the athlete taking a break from specific hockey-related training but maintaining a good fitness level. The transition period can be part of a regular season of play if breaks are included, such as in high school, college, and university leagues.

During the various training periods, give consideration to the development of technical (skill), tactical (team play), physical (conditioning), and psychological (mental) training programs. This book deals with drills for technical, tactical, and on-ice physical preparation.

Include in your planning monthly, weekly, and daily programs for the different macrocycles

An example of periodization (planning) for hockey would be:

APR	MAY JUN	JUL AUG	SEP OCT	NOV DEC JAN FEB	MAR
Transition	General Preparation	Specific Preparation	Pre-Competition	Competition Tapering*	Playoff

(NOTE: For further detailed information on periodization, refer to the book *Theory and Methodology of Training* by Tudor Bompa. Kendall/Hunt Publishing Co. 1985.)

* Tapering to occur one week to ten days at the end of February.

(training periods) for these main training periods. Important factors to consider are practice-to-game ratio and total amount of training time.

PLANNING THE PRACTICE

The individual practice is one part of the total plan. The development of individual skills (technical) as well as team play and systems (tactical) and conditioning should be part of each practice. In addition, you should address the strategy part of the game in each practice. As well as having a set plan for each practice, consider weaknesses you have observed in previous practices and games.

Plan the practice according to your philosophy of teaching related to the amount of activity and flow. Also consider the skill and physical development level of the athletes and confirm that the equipment and facilities are in proper order to ensure the safety of the players.

Make skill or technical development a part of most practices. A skill progression and suitable drills should be part of the plan; have a number of different drills to teach the same skill to prevent boredom. Systems and team play should be part of the tactical development of the practice. Make sure that systems such as breakouts and power plays fit the athletes' age and skill level, and progress from the simple to the more complex.

Include physical preparation (conditioning) in each practice. Take into account the conditioning effect of each skill drill and team drill when you design the practice. Consider such factors as development of the energy systems, strength, and flexibility.

Don't forget the mental aspect of practice. Include as part of the general practice plan tactics and strategy discussed and practiced during the training period.

Evaluate each practice after it has been completed and use this information to plan the next practice. Although you should plan for the whole year, your daily and weekly planning must be flexible enough to take in day-to-day changes to adjust to the strengths and weaknesses of the athletes and the team.

DESIGNING AN EFFECTIVE PRACTICE

1. Set the goals and objective of the practice. Inform the assistant coaches and players of what you are trying to accomplish.
2. Have a general progression throughout the practice from individual skills to team play.
3. Teach new skills and drills early in the practice.
4. Keep all players active and include the goaltenders in all drills.
5. Give clear, concise instructions throughout the practice and be in command.
6. Use effective teaching formations and make sure you have the attention of all athletes when you are speaking to them.
7. Explain and demonstrate skills and drills clearly. Put the players into the drills quickly after an explanation.
8. Don't talk too long at one time. Be concise, keeping to a one to one-and-a-half-minute explanation.
9. Inform your assistant coaches and use them effectively. Keep them active in all drills and make them part of everything you do.
10. Keep the players active and use all the ice surface. You may wish to use all the ice surface for team drills and divide the team up for some individual skill drills using different parts of the ice.

11. Observe, evaluate, and give feedback throughout the practice. Assistant coaches should be involved in this process as well.
12. Keep drills effective, competitive, active, and challenging.
13. Be positive and upbeat. Greet the athletes using their first names before practice or at the start of practice. Use voice communication throughout the practice at the proper times. Early in the practice, use voice communication more frequently to get the players going and establish a good rapport.
14. Include a warmup and cool-down in each practice. The warmup should include stretching and skating, and the cool-down should follow the reverse order of the warmup.
15. Use mass stretching and/or a skating fun warmup drill to get the team together and ready for the main part of the practice.
16. Include a fun drill in most practices.
17. Stop the drills when a general error or a lack of effort is apparent.
18. Choose drills for their conditioning features or have a conditioning drill or drills at the end of practice.
19. Speak to players as a group at the end of practice. Discuss the practice, upcoming games, general information, etc.
20. If time permits, have certain players work on specific skills with the assistant coaches after practice.
21. If possible, after practice have an off ice conditioning area for strength, anaerobic, and aerobic conditioning.
22. Conduct individual meetings with players before or after practices if time permits.
23. Meet with assistant coaches and possibly the captains to discuss and evaluate the practice and plan for the next practice or game.
24. Demand excellence. Repeat until the players get it right.

DESIGNING EFFECTIVE DRILLS

The development, designing, and implementing of effective drills is a key ingredient in coaching. How the athletes relate to the coach is in many ways directly related to how the drills and practices are implemented. The coach's knowledge, planning, and communication skills are very evident in the training sessions. How you practice is how you play. Effective, well-run drills are the essence of training.

Some guidelines for coaches in developing drills:
1. The drill should have a specific purpose and meet the objectives you have set for the practice.
2. The drill should be suitable to the age, skill level, and physical maturity (i.e., strength, size) of the athletes.
3. The drills should be applicable to the skills used in the game. Running a drill that does not relate to the skills used in the game and does not serve any purpose is meaningless to both the athlete and the coach.
4. Drills should follow a progression, moving from the simple to more complex. Build on previous drills, and develop a progression of drills for each skill taught.
5. Maximum participation of all the players should be an objective of every drill. All players should be involved in the drills and the number of trials or expectation of each skill should be at the maximum with only an adequate pause for recovery between trials or repetitions.
6. Drills should challenge the skill level of the athletes. If drills are too easy, the athletes will become bored quickly. Conversely, if the drills are too difficult, the athletes will become frustrated with lack of success.
7. Explain the drill clearly and demonstrate it before the athletes practice it. Your explanation should be clear, concise and, with the demonstration, should take less than three minutes.
8. Explain new drills in the dressing room using a rink diagram or on the ice using a rink board attached to the side glass. New drills may have to be demonstrated on the ice as well, especially if the drill is complex. In general, younger athletes need both an explanation and a demonstration while older, higher skilled athletes may need only a verbal explanation.
9. Drills should be varied and innovative. You should have a series of drills and a number of different ways of accomplishing the same purpose (e.g., one-on-one, two-on-one, etc.). Always be aware of new drills and be

innovative in designing drills. With older mature athletes, you may wish to combine a number of skills and purposes in one drill.

10. Drills should be undertaken at a tempo that simulates the action in the game. Practices with a high intensity are more enjoyable for the athletes and provide a carry-over into the game situation. Teams that practice at high tempo play at high tempo. Exceptions would be a drill that introduces a complex skill and thus must be broken down into parts and practiced initially at a slower speed until the skill is perfected.

11. It might seem obvious, but the drills should be done correctly. After you give a clear explanation and demonstration, you have the responsibility to see that the drill is done correctly. If the execution is not correct, stop the drill and emphasize the correct method.

12. The athletes should work with intensity in every drill. Inform the players of the intensity and work ethic required and remind them that it is the responsibility of the players and the coach that this work intensity be evident in all drills.

13. It is your responsibility as coach to give effective and constructive feedback during and after a drill is completed. The feedback can be general to all the players and/or specific to certain players. Athletes need to know how they are doing, and only with effective feedback can they correct the errors in their execution of a skill or drill. A complete understanding of the skills and the ability to observe and analyze are areas that all coaches must work on to become more proficient.

14. As much as possible, introduce competition into drills. Any time a race, a battle, or a winner is involved in a drill, the participants' interest and intensity levels are raised. As much as possible, you should try to equalize the competition when there is a large discrepancy in the skill level, size, and strength of the players.

15. Remain flexible in the development and running of drills. Some drills may be too complicated and have to be changed; other drills may not work with certain age groups. Stop drills or improvise when drills are not working.

16. Drills should run for the ideal amount of time – generally, they should not last longer than eight

to ten minutes and should be no shorter than three minutes. Coaches should be alert during a drill and not allow the drill to drag on. On the other hand, too short a drill will not allow enough repetitions for each player. The timing of a drill is a skill that develops with your experience and close observation of the intensity of the athletes while they perform the drill.

17. Drills should flow from one to another with a minimum of time between drills. Drills built on a progressional flow make an effective practice when put together. A well-planned drill progression gives an overall flow to the practice.

18. The whole ice surface should be used for most drills. The ideal drill has all players involved using the complete ice surface. In some situations, the players may be split into groups executing different drills on different sections of the ice surface.

19. If drills are planned correctly and executed at high tempo and a proper work-to-rest ratio is used, a conditioning effect should take place. Incorporate into each drill the number of repetitions along with the appropriate rest period for best results.

20. Drills should be enjoyable. Well-planned drills will allow the athletes to enjoy a practice. Make specific fun drills part of every practice.

21. Each drill should be evaluated after each practice. Did the drill accomplish its objective? Was the drill too difficult or too easy? Was the drill too long or too short? Was the drill executed properly? Did all players understand the drill? Were the players motivated throughout the drill? Were there noticeable improvements in the skill level?

22. Use drills that will improve areas of weakness evident in a previous game or practice. A certain drill may be more effective after a weakness was shown in a game. For example, a defensive-zone drill may be necessary at the practice after a game in which there was poor defensive execution. Certain specific skill drills such as shooting or checking may be appropriate after a game in which these skills were performed poorly.

23. Overall effective drills should show improvement in individual skills and team play. Teams

play as they practice. Individuals and teams should be evaluated on improvement, and effective, properly executed drills should make this improvement possible.

TYPES OF PRACTICES

Before establishing the type of practice you want to run, you need to know the amount of ice time available to you. Ideally, you should have at least one and a half hours of ice time, but in many cases you may find you have only one hour or only half the ice available. The effective use and planning of drills is even more important when ice time is limited.

Practices generally are of six types:
    General Skill
    Offensive
    Defensive
    Special Teams (Power Play and Penalty Killing)
    Fun
    Simple (No Brainer)

A general skill practice is a typical practice that includes skill development and some team play. This practice includes drills such as skill, offensive and defensive team play, and conditioning and is the most common type of practice.

An offensive practice has a theme of passing, moving the puck quickly and scoring, and generally raising the players' level of offensive skills. The drills have a high tempo with little resistance.

A defensive practice has the theme of forechecking, backchecking, and defensive team play. Some teams have this type of practice once a week if a number of practices are available. If a team is suffering from poor defensive play, this practice can get the players focused on the defensive aspect of the game.

Special team practices in such aspects of the game as power plays and penalty killing are important and usually effective the day before a game because they tend not to be exhaustive. These special practices are very important in the game of hockey and should be held at least once a week. If practice time is limited, aspects of this practice have to be incorporated in general practice.

Fun and simple (no brainer) practices have their place and can be used when the players appear fatigued or need a change of routine. Fun drills in a practice or a whole practice devoted to fun definitely have their place in a long season. A simple (no brainer) practice is one where little thinking is involved; no strategy or tactics are included and drills with little or no resistance are used. These practices should be short and included for the same reasons as a fun practice.

When the number of practices per week is limited, some aspects of the different types of practices may be included in one practice. An example of this type of practice would be to include defensive and special teams work in a general skill practice.

TYPICAL PRACTICE

1. Dressing-room stretch – Possible instruction 10 minutes before the practice
2. On-ice warmup – Skating warmup – Group fun – two pucks
3. Stretch together
4. Goalie warmup
5. One-on-zero, two-on-zero
6. One-on-one
7. Two-on-one
8. Three-on-one
9. Breakouts with regroups
10. Short scrimmage – instructional
11. Conditioning drills
12. Cool-down
13. Final group discussions

Post-practice: aerobic exercises, strength training

3

Teaching Progressions

Suggested Progressions for:

SKATING

PUCK CONTROL

PASSING AND RECEIVING

SHOOTING

CHECKING

GOALTENDING

BREAKOUTS

REGROUPS

OFFENSIVE ZONE PLAY

DEFENSIVE TEAM PLAY

POWER PLAY

PENALTY KILLING

FACE-OFFS

Complex skills are most easily acquired a bit at a time. The following is a suggested order for teaching skating, puck control, passing and receiving, shooting, checking, and goaltending. In addition, a general progression for teaching team skills, including breakouts, neutral zone regroups, offensive zone play and defensive team play, power play, penalty killing, and face-offs is presented.

The progressions are organized in order from simple to complex. In team drills, progressions range from no resistance or opposition to full opposition and resistance.

TEACHING PROGRESSION: SKATING

Forward skating
1. Skating stride
2. Front start
3. Side start
4. Two-foot stop
5. One-foot stop

Backward skating
1. Skating stride
2. Start
3. Two-foot stop
4. One-foot stop

Forward skating
1. Tight turn
2. Crossovers

Backward skating
1. Crossovers

Turning
1. Forward to backward
2. Backward to forward, heel-to-heel, crossover (Mohawk)
3. Backward to forward, with no stop

TEACHING PROGRESSION: PUCK CONTROL

Stick handling – front, side, diagonal
1. Stationary
2. Moving around cones
3. Moving around stationary players
4. One-on-one in a confined space

Deking
1. Fake one way, go the other – forehand
2. Fake one way, go the other – backhand
3. Change of speed
4. Stop and start
5. Curl
6. Stick fakes – pass or shoot
7. Between stick blade and skates – triangle
8. Between legs

Deking progression
1. Moving around a cone
2. Moving around a stationary player, one-on-one
3. Moving around a moving player, one-on-one

TEACHING PROGRESSION: PASSING

Passing skills
1. Forehand sweep pass
2. Backhand sweep pass
3. Drop pass
4. Back pass
5. Bank pass
6. Forehand snap pass
7. Backhand snap pass
8. Saucer forehand pass
9. Saucer backhand pass

Passing skills progression
1. Work in pairs, stationary
2. Work in pairs, moving

TEACHING PROGRESSION: PASS RECEIVING

Pass reception skills
1. Forehand
2. Backhand
3. Extended stick
4. Receiving the puck on the inside skate
5. Receiving the puck on the outside skate
6. Receiving the puck in the air with the glove
7. Receiving the puck in the air with the stick

Pass reception progression
1. Work in pairs, stationary
2. Work in pairs, moving
3. Three, four, and five players

TEACHING PROGRESSION: SHOOTING

Shooting skills
1. Forehand sweep shot
2. Backhand sweep shot
3. Forehand snap shot
4. Backhand snap shot
5. Forehand flip shot
6. Backhand flip shot
7. Slap shot
8. Shooting without stopping the puck (one-timers)

Shooting skills progression
1. Stationary, shooting against the boards
2. Moving, shooting against the boards
3. Moving, against the goaltender
4. Shooting after receiving the pass, against the goaltender

TEACHING PROGRESSION: CHECKING

Checking skills
1. Angling
2. Poke check
3. Sweep check
4. Stick lift and stick press
5. Taking a check
6. Shoulder check
7. Stick lift and shoulder check
8. Roller check (rotate opponent's shoulders towards boards)
9. Hook check
10. Diving poke check

Checking skills progression
1. Work in pairs, half-speed
2. Work in pairs, full-speed

TEACHING PROGRESSION: GOALTENDING

Goaltending skills
1. Stance
2. Side-to-side, in and out skating
3. Playing angles
4. Glove save
5. Blocker save
6. Half splits
7. Full splits
8. Up and down
9. Controlling rebounds
10. Double leg save
11. Clearing the puck
12. Blocking a pass from the corner
13. Stopping the puck behind the net
14. Screen shots
15. Freezing the puck with the glove

TEACHING PROGRESSION: BREAKOUT

1. Five vs. zero
2. Five vs. one
3. Five vs. two
4. Five vs. three
5. Five vs. five

TEACHING PROGRESSION: NEUTRAL ZONE REGROUP

1. Horseshoe
2. One forward with one defenceman
3. Two forwards with one defenceman
4. Two forwards with two defencemen
5. Three forwards with two defencemen
6. Three forwards with one defence pair, then another defence pair
7. Breakout with one regroup
8. Breakout with two regroups

TEACHING PROGRESSION: OFFENSIVE ZONE PLAY

Two-on-zero
1. Drive for the net
2. Crossing
3. Back pass
4. Bank pass
5. Curl (delay)
6. Quiet zone (cycling using backward board passes)

Three-on-zero
1. Offensive triangle
2. Drive for net – one, two, three principle
3. Center slow or stop, wingers drive for net
4. Center cross with winger
5. Bank pass
6. Curl (delay)
7. Quiet zone (cycling)
8. Pass back

Offensive zone progression
1. Two-on-one
2. Three-on-one
3. Three-on-two

TEACHING PROGRESSION: DEFENSIVE TEAM PLAY

1. Forechecking with one, two, and three forecheckers
2. Backchecking with one, two, and three backcheckers
3. Defensive zone coverage, five-on-five, no sticks
4. Defensive zone coverage, five-on-five, turn sticks
5. Defensive zone coverage, five-on-five, high tempo

TEACHING PROGRESSION: POWER PLAY

Offensive zone
1. One defenceman, one forward
2. One defenceman, two forwards
3. One defenceman, three forwards

4. Five-on-zero, five-on-two, five-on-three, five-on-four

5. Power-play breakout five-on-zero, five-on-two, five-on-three, five-on-four

TEACHING PROGRESSION: PENALTY KILLING

1. Four-on-zero, three-on-zero, defensive movement
2. Five-on-four, five-on-three, no sticks
3. Five-on-four, five-on-three, turn sticks
4. Five-on-three, game speed
5. Five-on-four, game speed

TEACHING PROGRESSION: FACE-OFFS

1. One-on-one
2. Three-on-three (forwards only)
3. Five-on-five

Part 2
Inspiration

4
Slogans for Success

SLOGANS FOR SUCCESS

When you can't change the direction of the wind, adjust your sails.

When giving advice, it's best to make it brief.

Encouragement from a good coach can turn an athlete's life around.

Most things important to know are difficult to learn.

Conscience and reason will have the last word. Passion will have the last deed.
Sigmund Freud

Don't judge those who try and fail. Judge only those who fail to try.

Behold the turtle. He makes progress only when he sticks his neck out.

The great challenge of life is to decide what's important and to disregard everything else.

A diamond is a chunk of coal that made good under pressure.

It's not hard to make decisions when you know what your values are.

You see things that are and say, "Why?" But you dream things that never were and say, "Why not?"

Praise in public, criticize in private.

Be humble – a lot was accomplished before you were born.

Don't be afraid to take big steps. You can't cross a chasm in two small jumps.

Challenges can be stepping stones or stumbling blocks. It's just a matter of how you view them.

Even if you are on the right track, you'll get run over if you just sit there.

When bad times come, you can let them make you bitter or use them to make you better.

Every great achievement was once considered impossible.

In the confrontation between the stream and the rock, the stream always wins – not through strength but by perseverance.

In the game of life, even the 50-yard seats don't interest me. I came to play.

Dream what you dare to dream. Go where you want to go. Be what you want to be.

The only limits are those of vision.

They can who believe they can.

Accept the challenges so that you may feel the exhilaration of victory.

Success is a dream turned into reality.

Some people dream of worthy accomplishments, while others stay awake and do them.

Success is a journey, not a destination.

Attitude is a little thing that makes a big difference.

The race is not always to the swift, but to those who keep running.

No one can predict to what heights you can soar. Even you will not know until you spread your wings.

Keep your face to the sunshine and you cannot see the shadows.

In the middle of every difficulty lies opportunity.

You cannot discover new oceans unless you have the courage to lose sight of the shore.

Do not fear the winds of adversity. Remember: A kite rises against the wind rather than with it.

Pride is a personal commitment. It is an attitude that separates excellence from mediocrity.

Excellence is the exceptional drive to exceed expectations.

In the end, the only people who fail are those who do not try.

When you lose, don't lose the lesson.

I've learned that you never get rewarded for the things that you intended to do.

I've learned that I still have a lot to learn.

Learn to listen. Opportunity sometimes knocks very softly.

Strive for excellence, not perfection.

Remember that overnight success usually takes about 15 years.

Remember that winners do what losers don't want to.

What your mind can conceive and your heart can believe, your body can achieve.

The road to success is always under construction.

Luck is when preparation meets opportunity.

Failure isn't fatal and success isn't final.

Our greatest glory is not in never falling, but in rising every time we fall.

Most things are difficult before they are easy.

The difference between playing to win and playing not to lose is often the difference between success and mediocrity.

Winners see what they want to happen. Losers see what they want to avoid.

When you lose say little. When you win say less.

You play a game with the head and heart.

It is better to try and fail than to fail to try.

Your attitude will determine your altitude.

We are what we repeatedly do. Excellence, then, is not an act, but a habit
Aristotle

You can't build a reputation on what you are going to do.

An idea is only as good as its execution.

Giving up reinforces a sense of incompetence. Going on gives you a commitment to succeed.

Only those who have the patience to do simple things perfectly will acquire the skill to do difficult things easily.

Winners see what they want to happen. Losers see what they want to avoid.

Most people fail not because they aim too high – but because they aim at nothing.

All people are created with an equal opportunity to become unequal.

Doing the best that you are capable of is victory, and doing less is defeat.

Be thankful for adversity – it separates the winners from the quitters.

You are what you are when no one is around.

Remember when you are not practicing, somewhere someone is and when you meet him, he will win.

Those who profit most are those who give the most.

When a winner makes a mistake, he says, "I was wrong"; when a loser makes a mistake, he says, "It wasn't my fault."

A winner credits good luck for winning, even though it isn't good luck. A loser blames bad luck for losing even though it isn't bad luck.

A winner never quits. A quitter never wins.

When the going gets tough, the tough get going.

The amount of success you are able to achieve through wisdom will be in direct proportion to the effort expended in acquiring it.

A nice thing about the future is that it comes one day at a time.

The trouble with not having a goal is that you can spend your life running up and down the field and never score.

You cannot push someone up the ladder unless he is willing to climb himself.

Whatever the mind can conceive and believe, it can achieve.

Attitude is an inner concept. It is the most important thing you can develop in your life.
Wayne Dyer

Nothing ever built arose to touch the skies unless some man dreamed that it should, some man believed that it could, and some man willed that it must.
Charles Kettering

To do what others cannot do is talent. To do what talent cannot do is genius.
Will Henry

Strange how much you got to know before how little you know.
Duncan Stuart

He didn't know it couldn't be done … so he did it.

Nothing great was ever achieved without enthusiasm.
Ralph Waldo Emerson

To be what we are, and to become what we are capable of becoming is the only end of life.
Robert Louis Stevenson

The reward of a task well done is in being called to do a bigger one.

Once in a century a man may be ruined or made insufferable by praise. But surely, once in a minute, something generous dies for want of it.
Erich Fromm

In the long run, people hit only what they aim at. Therefore, they had better aim at something high.
Henry David Thoreau

Press on: nothing in the world can take the place of persistence. Talent will not; nothing is more common than unsuccessful individuals with talent. Genius will not; unrewarded genius is almost a proverb. Education will not; the world is full of educated derelicts. Persistence and determination alone are important. The slogan "press on" has solved, and always will solve, the problems of the human race.

We see obstacles when we take our eyes off our goals.

Every noble work is at first impossible.
Thomas Carlyle

Chance favours the prepared mind.
Louis Pasteur

Life does not require that we become the biggest or the best, only that we try.

They won because they refused to become discouraged by their defeats.

He can who thinks he can, and he can't who thinks he can't. This is an inexorable, indisputable law.
Orison Marden

The only thing that stands between a man and what he wants from life is often merely the will to try it and the faith to believe that it is possible.
Richard Devos

The first and most important step toward success is the feeling that we can succeed.
Nelson Boswell

A man is literally what he thinks.
James Allen

The only limit to our realization of tomorrow will be our doubts of today.
Franklin Roosevelt

The barrier between success is not something which exists in the real world; it is composed purely and simply of doubts about ability.
Mark Caine

Failure is the only opportunity to move intelligently to begin again.
Henry Ford

The greatest mistake a man can make is to be afraid of making one.
Elbert Hubbard

The difference between greatness and mediocrity is often how an individual views a mistake.
Nelson Boswell

No man fails who does his best.
Orison Marden

If you don't know where you are going, how can you expect to get there?
Basil Walsh

The only limits, as always, are those of vision.
James Broughton

Success doesn't come to you ... you go to it.
Marua Collins

If it is meant to be, it is up to me.
Sherry Bassin

Whether you think you can or think you can't – you are right.
Henry Ford

In order to succeed we must first believe we can.
Michael Korda

I found that I could find the energy, that I could find the determination to keep on going. I learned that your mind can amaze your body, if you just keep telling yourself, I can do it, I can do it, I can do it.
Jon Erickson

We can do only what we think we can do. We can be only what we think we can be. We can have only what we think we can have. What we do, what we are, what we have, all depend upon what we think.
Robert Collier

He who loses wealth loses much; he who loses a friend loses more; he who loses courage loses all.
Cervantes

Courage is resistance to fear, mastery of fear – not absence of fear.
Mark Twain

What the superior man seeks is in himself: what the small man seeks is in others.
François La Rouchefoucauld

SLOGANS FOR LEADERSHIP

Leaders are like eagles. They don't flock – you find them one at a time.

Leadership is an attitude before it is an ability.

The speed of the leader determines the rate of the pack.

Real leaders are ordinary people with extraordinary determination.

Be a leader: Remember the lead sled dog is the only one with a decent view.

Accept the fact that regardless of how many times you are right, you will sometimes be wrong.

Be decisive even if it means you'll sometimes be wrong.

Don't use time or words carelessly. Neither can be retrieved.

I believe some of us must assume leadership, I believe young people thirst to be led to better themselves. Life is hard and success is survival. Leaders inspire us. Leaders show us the way.
Frank Leahy, college football coach

You don't become a leader because you say you are. It's much more what you do than what you say.
Sparky Anderson, professional baseball coach

A successful leader has to be innovative. If you are not one step ahead of the crowd, you soon will be a step behind everyone else.
Tom Landry, professional football coach

The players don't want to see me rushing around and screaming. They want to believe I know what I am doing.
Tom Landry, professional football coach

If it doesn't work, I'll take the blame. You need that courage to be a good coach.
John McKay, professional football coach

If you set up an atmosphere of communication and trust, it becomes a tradition. Older team members will establish your credibility with newer ones. Even if they don't like everything about you, they'll still say, "He's trustworthy, committed to us as a team."
Mike Krzyzewski, college basketball coach

SLOGANS FOR TEAMWORK

Coming together is a beginning; keeping together is progress; working together is success.
Henry Ford

Teamwork is the ability to work together toward a common vision, the ability to direct individual accomplishment toward organizational objectives. It is the fuel that allows common people to attain uncommon results.

Teamwork is the collective talents of many individuals.

It's amazing what a team can accomplish when no one cares who gets the credit.
John Wooden, college basketball coach

Together everyone achieves more.

Two stone cutters were asked what they were doing. The first said, "I'm cutting this stone into blocks. The second replied, "I'm on a team that's building a cathedral."

There is no I in the word team.

When you come to practice, you cease to exist as an individual. You're part of a team.
John Wooden, college basketball coach

Are you playing for your name in the paper, or your name on the trophy?
Sherry Bassin, Manager,
junior and professional hockey

Are you playing for the name on the back of your sweater or the name on the front of the sweater?
Sherry Bassin

SPORT QUOTATIONS

Life is 10% what happens to me and 90% how I react to it.
Lou Holtz, college football coach

I always turn to the sports page first . . . it records people's accomplishments, the front page nothing but man's failure.
Earl Warren, former chief justice
United States Supreme Court

In baseball and in business, there are three types of people. There are those who make it happen, those who watch it happen, and those who wonder what happened.
Tommy Lasorda, professional baseball coach

We aren't where we want to be, we aren't where we ought to be, but thank goodness we aren't where we used to be.
Lou Holtz, college football coach

When you think of the Forty-Niners, you think of their tradition. When you think of all the good teams of the past, like the old Steelers, the old Raiders, they all had identity. We will have identity. We want men who will stand up and be counted. Men who will make something happen.
Jerry Glanville, professional football coach

If you accept losing, you can't win.
Vince Lombardi, professional football coach

Confidence comes from hours and days and weeks and years of constant work and dedication.
Roger Staubach, former professional football player

There is no substitute for work. It is the price of success.
Earl Blaik, college football coach

Winning isn't everything, but making the all-out effort to win is the most important thing.
Vince Lombardi, professional football coach

I will demand a commitment to excellence and to victory and that is what life is all about.
Vince Lombardi, professional football coach

Failure is good. It's fertilizer. Everything I've learned about coaching I've learned by making mistakes.
Rick Pitino, college basketball coach

How you select people is more important than how you manage them once they're on the job. If you start with the right people you won't have problems later on.
Red Auerbach, general manager,
professional basketball

We're probably the most careful hirers of employees that you've ever met. We follow the Carpenter's Rule. . . . Measure twice and cut once, except we measure about four or five times and hire once.
Dan Finanne, president, professional basketball team

It's what you learn after you know it all that counts.
John Wooden, college basketball coach

If you recruit good players and they play well, you're a genius. . . . So for a year or two you'll be called a genius. Sometimes a "genius manager" will recruit bad players, who play poorly, which will make people wonder how come a genius got so dumb so fast.
Whitey Herzog, professional baseball coach

A team should be an extension of the coach's personality. My teams are arrogant and obnoxious.
Al McGuire, college basketball coach

You have to improve your club, even if it means letting your own brother go.
Tim McCarver, former baseball player

People are human. If you're going to criticize them, compliment them first.
Bum Phillips, professional football coach

Deep down, your players must know you care about them. This is the most important thing. I could never get away with what I do if the players felt I didn't care. They know in the long run, I'm in their corner.
Bo Schembechler, college football coach

A lifetime contract for a coach means, if you're ahead the third quarter, moving the ball, they can't fire you.
Lou Holtz, college football coach

There are certain things in this world we all have in common, such as time. Everybody has sixty seconds to a minute, sixty minutes to an hour, twenty-four hours to a day; the difference is what we do with that time and how we use it.
Lou Holtz, college football coach

If you make every game a life-and-death proposition you're going to have problems. For one thing you'll be dead a lot.
Dean Smith, college basketball coach

Tackle your hardest job first. Usually when we are faced with a number of projects to work on, we take the easiest or the most rewarding one first. Start with a job you really don't want to do. Once you get it out of the way, everything else will seem easy.
Red Auerbach, general manager, professional basketball

There are certain qualities that you look for in people, whether you are on a football team or in business. You look for people who are committed, devoted and doing the best job. Talent isn't going to matter either. I'll take the guy who is out breaking his butt over a guy with talent in a close situation every time. I may get my butt beat a few times, but in the long run, I'll win because I'll have a guy with more character.
Mike Ditka, professional football coach

The will to prepare to win is infinitely more important than the will to win. A team that is really willing to prepare is the team that has the best chance to win and wants to win.
Bobby Knight, college basketball coach

Winning isn't everything, but it beats anything that comes in second.
Bear Bryant, college football coach

Sustain a family life for a long period of time and you can sustain success for a long period of time. First things first. If your life is in order, you can do whatever you want.
Pat Riley, professional basketball coach

Next year is not about winning another championship or having one more ring or developing bigger reputations. It's about leaving footprints.
Pat Riley, professional basketball coach

Success is not a sometimes thing. In other words, you don't do what is right once in awhile, but all the time. Success is a habit. Winning is a habit.
Vince Lombardi, professional football coach

The stylish graceful, accommodating, easy-going affable coach will get 80% of the job done. The final 20% can be directly attributed to making tough decisions, demanding a high standard of performance, meeting expectations, paying attention to details, and grabbing and shaking when necessary.
Bill Walsh, professional and college football coach

They may outsmart me, or be luckier, but they can't outwork me.
Woody Hayes, college football coach

Luck is what happens when preparation meets opportunity.
Darrell Royal, college football coach

If you're not playing well you're not going to play. That's the bottom line. The players are responsible for themselves and the reward or punishment is going to be whether they play or not. It's just that simple.
Pat Burns, professional hockey coach

Success is perishable and often outside our control. In contrast, excellence is something that's lasting, dependable and largely within a person's control.
Joe Paterno, college football coach

Part 3
The Drills

5
Skating

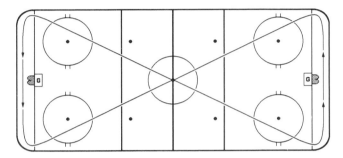

SK I

NOTE: These drills can be done skating backward or forward. Players skate around the rink going behind the goals, moving in both directions.

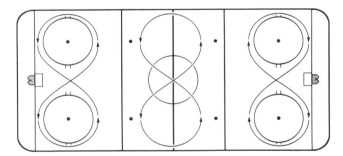

SK 2

Players skate a small figure "8" in all three zones.

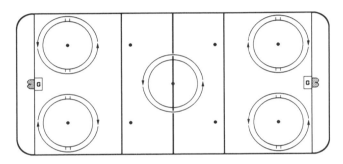

SK 3

Form the players into five groups. Change direction forward and backward using pivots. Use wide crossovers and all four edges.

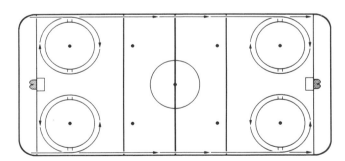

SK 4

Place players into two groups and skate the circles as shown. Skate both forward and backward.

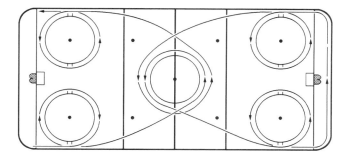

SK 5

All the players start from one corner. Skate both forward and backward. Keep your head up, especially when skating the center-ice circle.

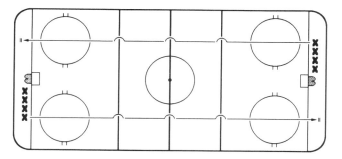

SK 6

Players develop balance by skating the length of the ice and executing jumps at the blue lines and the center red line. Perform the drill forward and backward.

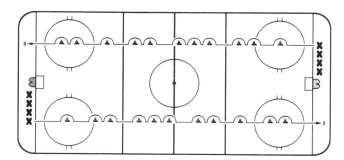

SK 7

Place pylons so that players can jump using short and long strides. Perform the drill at a slower speed for early success and increase the tempo when execution has improved.

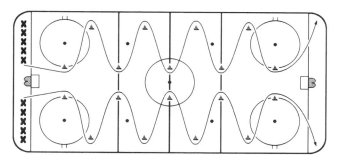

SK 8

Players skate the pylon course using tight turns. Do the drill forward and backward.
   Variation: Add pucks and shoot on the goal.

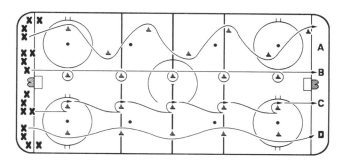

SK 9

(1) Place pylons in zig-zag pattern down the ice. Skate forward and backward through the pylons.
(2) Players skate forward and backward, clockwise and counter clockwise, around the pylons.
(3) Players deke each pylon using a sharp turn right and then left.
(4) Players skate forward and backward through the pylons, which are placed in a straight line.

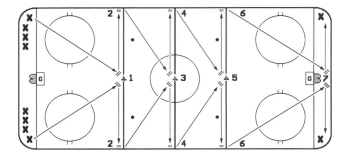

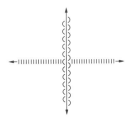

SK 10

All players skate forward, stopping at each pylon (1 to 7) up the ice. Each player leaves when the one ahead reaches the blue line. All players stay at one end when they complete the drill, then reverse direction.

Variation: All players skate forward to points 1, 3, 5, and 7 and backward to pylons 2, 4, and 6.

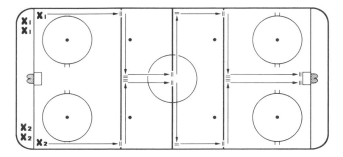

SK 11

X1 and X2 start at the same time. They follow the drill as shown, i.e., skate forward to the blue line, stop, forward to the center of the ice, stop, etc.

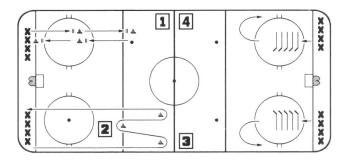

SK 12

Set up four stations as follows:
(1) Players skate forward and stop at each pylon.
(2) Players skate the course doing tight turns.
(3) Players use "V-start" and step over sticks.
(4) Players use crossover start and step over sticks.
Rotate groups throughout each station.

SK 13

On the coach's hand signs, players singly or as a group move forward, backward, and sideways. The players should keep their heads up and stay up on the toes.

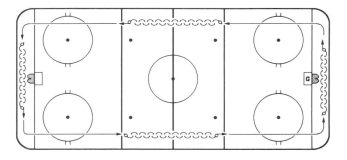

SK 14

The players skate forward around the perimeter of the rink. When the coach blows the whistle, they skate backward. Repeat. The players turn the opposite way each time in order to work on the pivot in both directions.

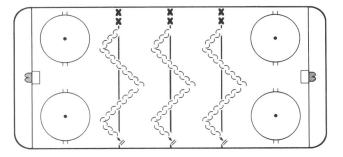

SK 15

Players skate backward, moving laterally side to side across the ice.

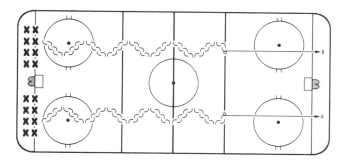

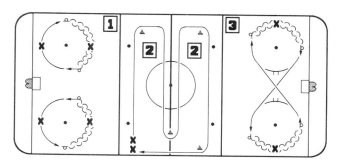

SK 16

Players skate backward and move laterally side to side depending on the coach's signal – left or right.

SK 19

(1) Two players are on each circle. Players must always pivot backward with outside shoulder facing in toward the face-off dot. They do the drill clockwise and counter-clockwise.
(2) Players skate the width of rink, doing crossovers and tight turns both forward and backward.
(3) They skate a figure "8" backward on the circles and forward between the circles.

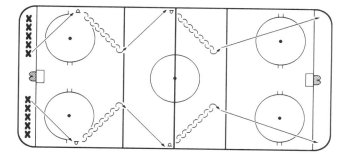

SK 17

Players skate forward to the hash marks, pivot, skate backward to the blue line, pivot, etc., following the pattern as outlined.

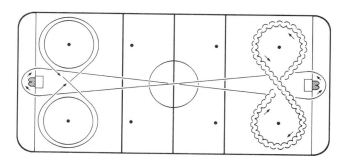

SK 20

Players skate the figure "8" around the goals and the circles, using forward and backward skating as indicated.

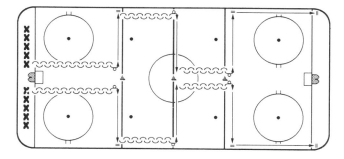

SK 18

Players skate the pattern as outlined: backward to the blue line, pivot, forward to the boards, stop, etc.

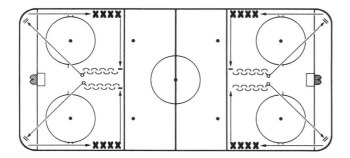

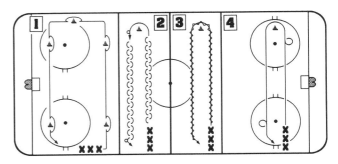

SK 21

Players skate forward (laterally) across the blue line, stop, skate backward to the top of the face-off circle, pivot, and skate to the corner. When they reach the corner, they stop and then skate forward to the back of the line.

NOTE: Groups should switch sides halfway through the drill to be sure they are working on stopping and turning using all edges.

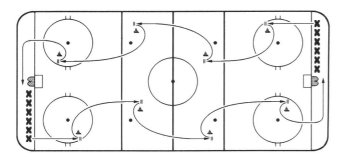

SK 24

(1) Players jump over an object while skating the course.

(2) Players skate backward the width of the ice, pivot just before the pylon, do a tight turn around the pylon, pivot, and skate backward from where they started.

(3) With a puck, players skate forward the width of the rink, do a tight turn around the pylon, and skate back from where they started.

(4) Players skate the width of the ice then roll over/tumble. After doing a tight turn around the pylon, they do the same, returning from where they came.

SK 22

Players skate the course, executing crossover starts after each stop. The crossover starts are performed both to the left and to the right.

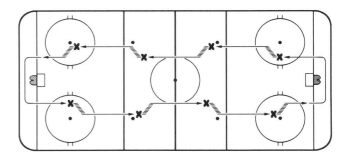

SK 25

Players skate around the rink, crossing over three steps to the left or three steps to the right, depending on the coach's signal. They should do the drill forward and backward both with and without pucks, starting slowly and building to a high tempo.

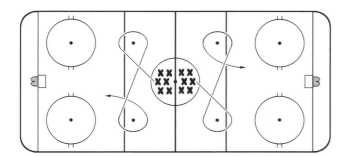

SK 23

Players skate out of the center circle and loop both face-off dots before driving to the net. Players should try to accelerate off the turns and sprint to the goal line.

Variation: Add pucks.

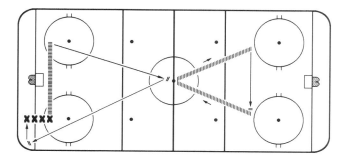

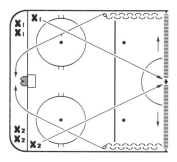

SK 26

Players start at the bottom of the circle, doing stepovers to the opposite circle. They skate forward to the center-ice dot, stop, do stepovers to the top of the circle, skate laterally (forward) across the ice to the top of the opposite circle, and stop. They do stepovers back to the center-ice dot, stop, and then skate forward to the starting line. They should do stepovers both ways.

SK 28

X1 and X2 start at the same time. They skate directly to the center-ice dot, stop, and do stepovers to the boards. On reaching the boards, they pivot, skate backward to the blue line, pivot, and skate forward to the back of the goal.

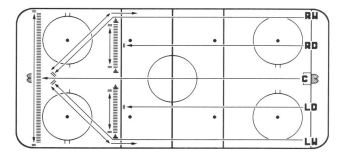

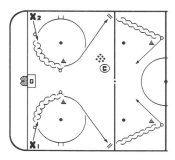

SK 27

Three forwards and two defencemen skate down the ice. The wingers cut at the far blue line and skate directly to the net and back to the blue line twice. The center skates to the goal crease and moves laterally side to side twice. The defencemen skate to the far blue line and cross-step to the pylons three times. After this, the players skate the length of the ice, returning to their starting point.

SK 29

X1 and X2 start at the same time. They skate out to the face-off circle, pivot, and skate backward around the circle to the inside hash marks. They then pivot and skate forward to the blue line, stop, skate backward around the neutral zone pylon, pivot again, and race for a puck on the blue line. The winner takes a shot on goal. The other player can act as a checker or be looking for a rebound.

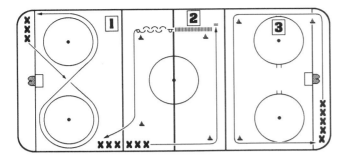

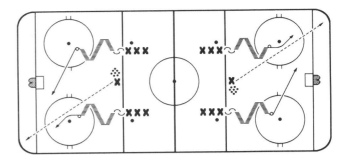

SK 30

(1) Players skate in a figure "8" using crossovers.
(2) Players skate forward from the blue line to the blue line and across the ice. Players stop at the far boards, then do stepovers to the center red line, pivot, skate backward to the blue line, pivot, and skate forward across the ice to the starting line.
(3) Players skate the outside square using tight turns on the corners.

SK 33

Players skate backward from the blue line. They take three steps to the outside, six steps to the inside, three steps to the outside, and then pivot and skate forward to the corner to retrieve the puck shot in by the coach while in the six-step movement.

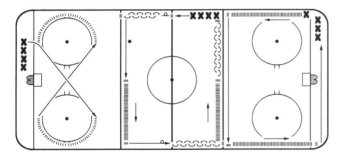

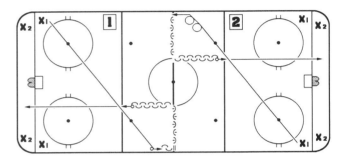

SK 31

Players execute stepovers in three zones using stepovers, forward skating, and backward skating as indicated.

SK 34

(1) Players start at the goal line, skate to the center red line at the boards, pivoting forward to backward just prior to reaching the red line. They stop at the center red line, do cariokas (right leg over left leg, left leg behind right leg, etc.) to the center-ice circle, pivot, skate backward to the blue line, pivot, and skate forward to the goal line.
(2) Same drill as (1) except players do two 360-degree circles (one each way) just prior to reaching the center red line.

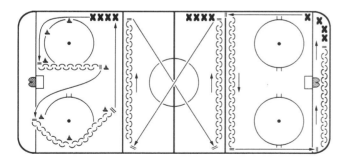

SK 32

Players skate three different courses, skating backward and stopping in the areas as shown.

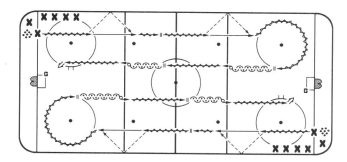

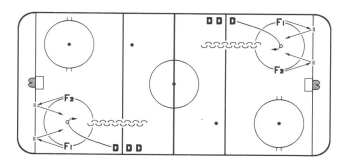

SK 35

The player starts skating with a puck, board-passes to himself, and stops once in possession of the puck. The player starts skating again and board-passes to himself at the far blue line, skates forward around the circle, and stops at the inside hash marks. The player then pivots and skates backward to the blue line, pivots, skates forward to the center red line, and stops. The player pivots again and skates backward to the blue line, pivots, and skates forward, finishing with a shot on goal. Use both sides of the ice at the same time and switch sides halfway through the drill.

SK 37

Put the defencemen on the boards as shown at approximately the top of the circles. The forwards are on the outside and inside hash marks, respectively. The forwards sprint to the goal line, stop, and sprint up-ice. The defencemen loop around the face-off dot and then skate backward, keeping the forwards in front. Use both sides of ice.

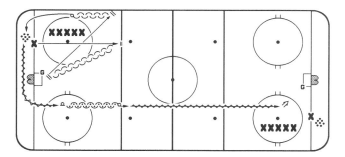

SK 36

The player skates to the blue line, stops, skates backward to the crease, forward to the blue line, and stops. X then skates backward to the hash marks, pivots, skates forward to the corner, and retrieves a puck. The player then skates behind the net and skates up the ice pivoting at the face-off dot, skating backward to the blue line, pivots, and skates forward to the far end for a shot on goal.

6
Puck Control

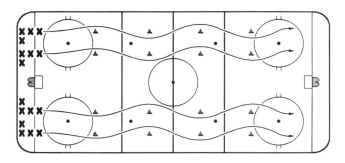

PC 1

The players skate down the ice skating between the pylons. Perform the drill without pucks first, then add pucks.

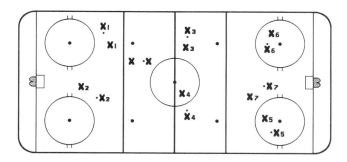

PC 2

Select pairs of players of equal size and ability. The player with the puck try to keep the puck away from their partner. Perform the drill for 30 to 40 seconds and then change positions. Perform the drill in a small area such as two pairs in a circle.

Variation: Have the checkers with their sticks upside down or no sticks at all.

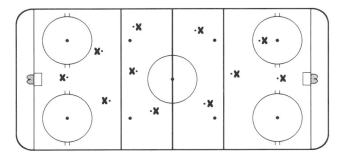

PC 3

Players skate around the ice stickhandling with one hand. They perform the drill first with the top hand, then with the bottom hand. Finally, they perform the drill with both hands, moving the puck left to right, right to left, forward to backward, etc.

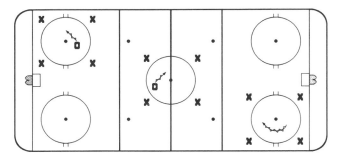

PC 4

The player in the middle skates around the circle stickhandling while four players standing on the circle try to poke-check the puck off the puck carrier's stick. The puck carriers should practice deking when poked at by the players on the circle.

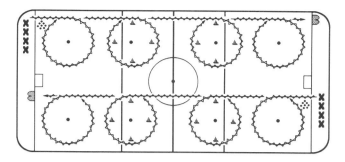

PC 5

Players skate around the circles as indicated and end up with a shot on goal. One side skates clockwise and the other side skates counter-clockwise.

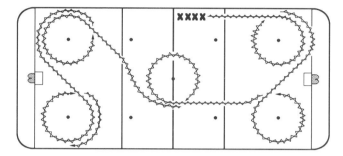

PC 6

The players skate the circles as indicated with a puck.

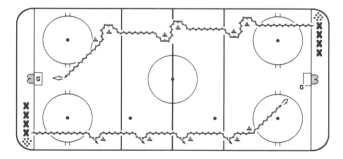

PC 7

The players skate down the right side of the ice, putting a head-and-shoulder fake at each pair of pylons. The drill finishes with a shot on goal. Players come down the other side of the ice deking outside/in or inside/out before shooting on goal.

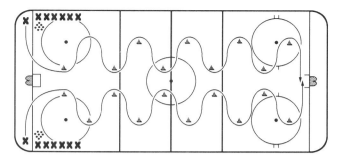

PC 8

Players skate around the ice as shown, doing tight turns while handling the puck. Use puck protection when doing the tight turns around the pylons.

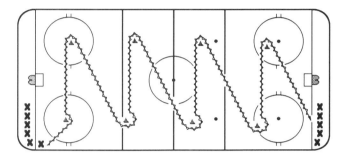

PC 9

The players skate around the pylons, finishing with a shot on goal. Practice tight turns, puck protection, etc.

Variation: Have a race. The winner is the player who completes the snake first.

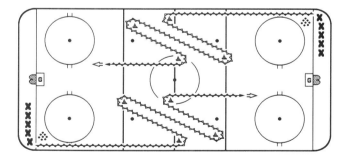

PC 10

The players start in both ends, skating through the course and using tight turns around the pylons, protecting the puck in the turns and accelerating coming out of the turns. They finish the drill with a shot on goal.

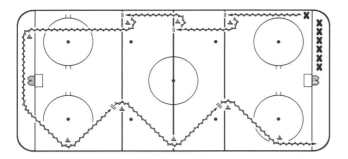

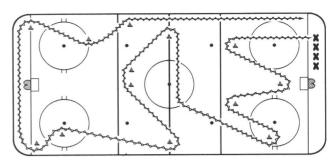

PC 11

The players skate the course and the pylons with a puck as shown. The players stop on both sides.

PC 14

The players skate the circuit shown.

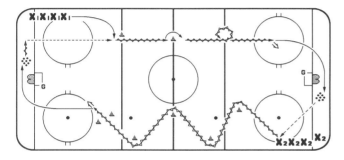

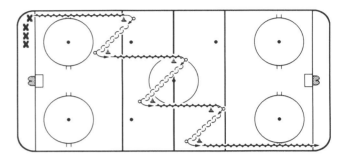

PC 12

To start the drill, have a player or coach make the first pass in each end. X1 skates towards the blue line, receives a pass, jumps over the pylon at center, does a 360-degree tight turn at the far blue line and then takes a shot on goal. X1 continues behind the goal where he picks up a puck and passes to X2 before going to the end of the X2 line. X2 skates as shown and takes a shot on goal. X2 then continues behind the goal, picks up a puck, and passes to X1 before joining the back of the X1 line.

PC 15

Players skate the course forward, then pivot, skate backward, then pivot, skate forward, etc. Players should skate the course without pucks first, then with pucks.

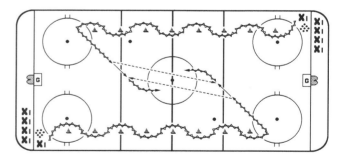

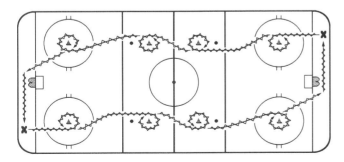

PC 16

Both players skate around the pylons and pass to each other in the center-lane area as shown. They finish with a shot on goal.

PC 13

The players skate the circles doing 360-degree turns at each pylon. Have them practice turns in each direction.

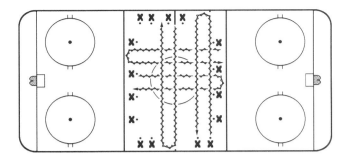

PC 17

Divide the players into four groups in the neutral zone as shown, with each player having a puck. On the coach's whistle, all the players on the boards skate to the opposite boards and back. At the same time, the players on the blue lines skate to the opposite blue line and back.

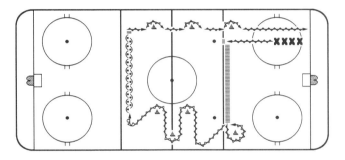

PC 18

The players skate as shown, doing crossovers at the first blue line.

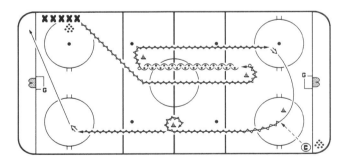

PC 19

The players skate the circuit with pucks forward and backward and take a shot on goal. They then receive a second puck on a pass from the coach and complete the circuit, finishing with another shot on goal.

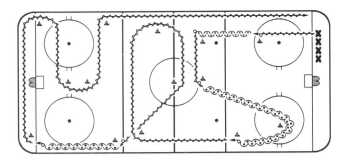

PC 20

The players skate as shown doing forward and backward skating with the puck.

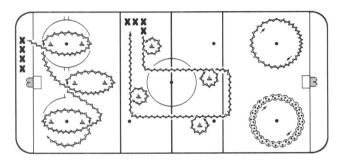

PC 21

Divide the players into three groups and have the players skate the different zones, skating as shown with the puck.

7
Passing

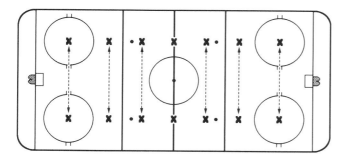

PS 1

The players should be close together, passing to each other using the forehand and backhand sweep pass. As players improve, lengthen the distance they have to pass.

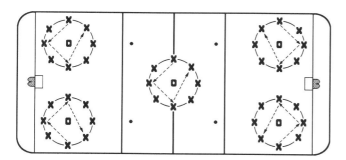

PS 2

The players pass the puck through the circle. The player in the middle must try and intercept the pass. If intercepted, the player in the middle is replaced by the player who made the pass.

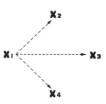

PS 3

The players do quick passing and receiving with X1. X1 receives the pass and moves the puck to the next in line. (X2 to X1 and X1 to X3; X3 to X1 and X1 to X4; X4 to X1 and X1 to X2.) Perform the drill for 15 seconds and rotate positions.

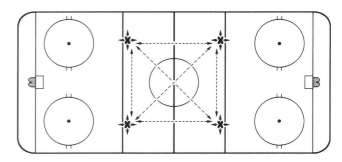

PS 4

Position four players as shown. The players move the puck around in a triangular formation.

Variation: Place two players in the middle to pressure the passer and pass receiver.

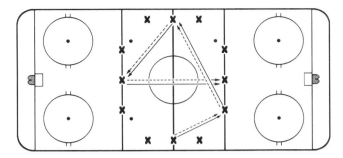

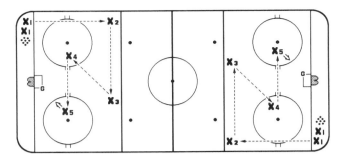

PS 5

Set up the players as shown. After passing, the player uses quick starts to race to where the puck was passed. With a large group (10 players) use two pucks.

PS 8

X1 starts the drill passing to X2, X2 to X3, etc. After the pass is made, the passer skates to the receiver's position.

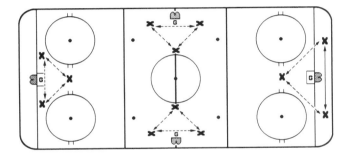

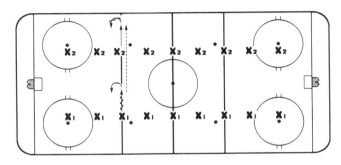

PS 6

Players move the puck around the net area in a triangle passing forward. If the goaltender is out of position after three passes, the player takes a shot on goal.

PS 9

Set up the players as shown. X1 passes the puck to a moving X2. After receiving the pass, X1 and X2 do tight turns and this time X2 passes to X1. The receivers should take the pass on their backhand sides. Go back and forth across the ice.

Variation: X1 skates forward while X2 is skating backward. As X2 nears the boards, X1 passes the puck to X2. X2 stops and starts forward while X1 pivots and skates backward. Go back and forth across the ice.

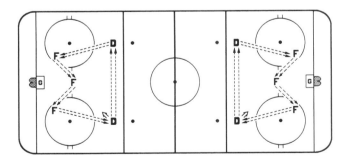

PS 7

The players pass the puck around the "W." The left defence starts the drill. After passing around twice, the left defence takes a shot on goal. The three forwards try for deflections, screens, and/or rebounds. Rotate positions after the shot.

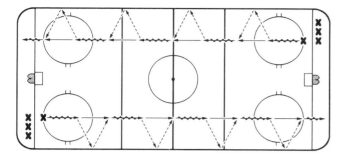

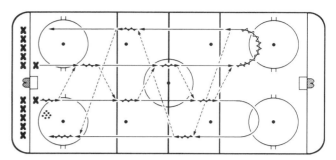

PS 10

Players skate the length of the ice, passing the puck to the boards and receiving the puck back. The players learn that the angle the puck hits the boards is the angle at which the puck will come back to them.

PS 13

The players skate the middle lane passing, turning, and making rink-wide passes on the way back.

Variation: Use two pucks.

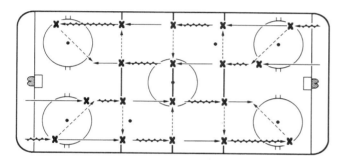

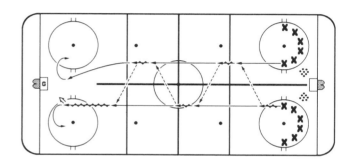

PS 11

The players skate around the ice, passing to each other on the forehand and the backhand. Perform the drill slowly at first and increase the speed after the players can pass accurately.

PS 14

Pairs of players skate up the ice, flip-passing over an obstacle (hockey sticks, a large rope, etc.). Players take a shot on goal as they complete the last pass. Perform both forehand and backhand passes.

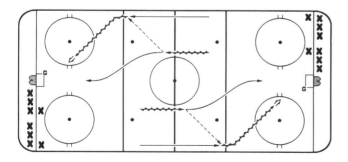

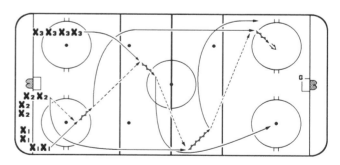

PS 12

The players skate down the ice, passing to each other with the outside player taking the shot on goal. The trailing player in the middle goes for the rebound.

Variation: The player in the middle receives the pass in the high slot from the player who went wide and deep with the puck.

PS 15

X1 cuts across to the middle, X2 passes to X1, and X2 fills the X1 lane. X1 passes to X3, cutting into the middle. X1 fills the X3 lane, etc. The players fill the lane that was left vacant and the player without the puck always cuts behind the player with the puck. Finish with a shot on goal.

Variation: Use two pucks.

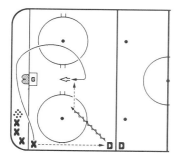

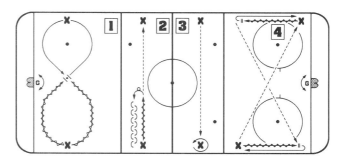

PS 16

Player X passes to the point. As soon as X passes to D, X skates behind the net and curls out to the high slot to receive a pass from D, who has moved into the circle and makes a quick pass.

PS 19

(1) Players skate the figure "8" with a drop pass in the middle.

(2) Players skate forward and pass, pivot, skate backward, and receive a pass.

(3) Players receive a pass, do a 360-degree turn and pass back.

(4) A player receives a pass, skates as shown, and passes diagonally to a teammate. After the pass, the player skates down to the goal line.

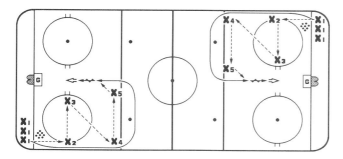

PS 17

X1 makes the first pass and then skates to be in position to receive a pass back from X5 in the high slot for a shot on goal.

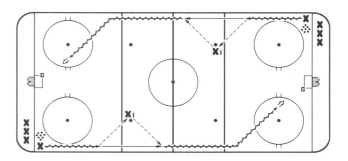

PS 20

The player with the puck passes to X1 or the coach on the face-off dot. X1 returns the pass to X. Finish with a shot on goal.

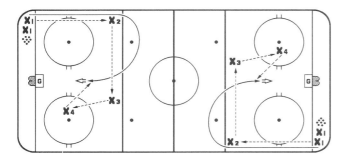

PS 18

X1 passes to X2, X2 to X3, and X3 to X4. X4 feeds a slot pass to X1, who chases the first pass to X2 position and then cuts down through the middle. Rotate positions in order of numbers.

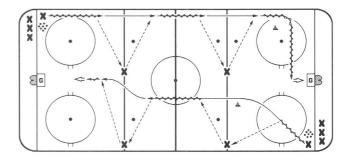

PS 21

X does a double give-and-go down the boards and a give-and-go in the middle lane. The drill finishes with a shot on goal.

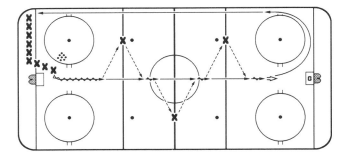

PS 22

The players skate up the middle of the ice, making three give-and-go passes before finishing with a shot on goal. Rotate the pass receivers.

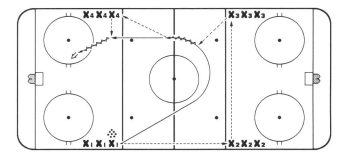

PS 23

X1 passes to X2, who passes to X3. X1 skates around the center circle and receives a return pass. X3 does a give-and-go with X4 and shoots. X3 starts next with a pass to X4, etc.

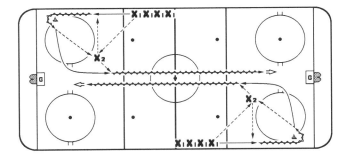

PS 24

X1 passes to X2. X2 touch-passes back to X1 before turning around the pylon. X1 passes to X2 again and X2 touch-passes back to X1, who has a breakaway on goal.

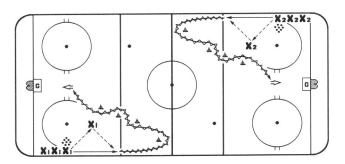

PS 25

X1 does a basic give-and-go, skates into the neutral zone, and stickhandles through the pylons before taking a shot on goal. Use the drill in both ends of the ice.

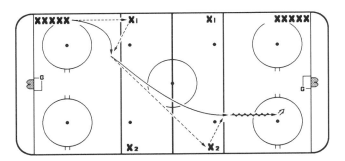

PS 26

X starts the drill with a give-and-go pass to X1. X then makes a diagonal pass to X2 for another give-and-go. Players from both ends go at the same time.

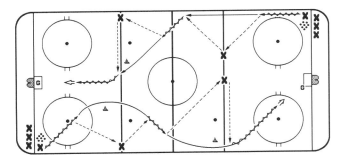

PS 27

X makes two passes through the middle for a return pass and drives to the net for a shot on goal.

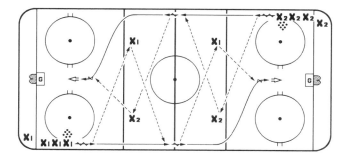

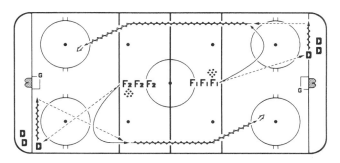

PS 28

X1 and X2 in the corners start by passing to partners on the neutral-zone face-off dots. X1 pass to X1 and X2 pass to X2 until a shot on goal. Change passers at face-off dots halfway through drill.

PS 31

F1 passes to D1, who skates towards the boards and passes back to a curling F1. F1 then skates the length of the ice for a shot on goal. At the same time, F2 passes to D2, who skates towards the goal and reverse passes to a curling F2, who skates the length of the ice for a shot on goal.

PS 29

X1 is by the boards at the top of the circle with X2 positioned at the bottom of the circle. X3 and X4 are at the two blue lines. X2 does a give-and-go with X1 and shoots. X2 then receives a pass from X3, does a give-and-go with X3 and X4 and shoots.

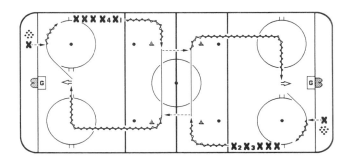

PS 32

X1 starts with a puck and X2 starts without a puck. X1 passes to X2, who skates in and takes a shot on goal. X1 skates across the ice below the center red line and receives a pass from X3, who is about three seconds behind X2. After the shot, the players skate to the corner, receive a pass out, and join the line.

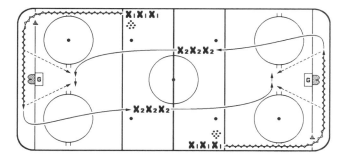

PS 30

X1 carries the puck into the corner and behind the net. X1 passes to X2 on the hash marks. X1 can pass to the left or right hash marks and X2 must position accordingly.

Variation: Have two players on the hash marks.

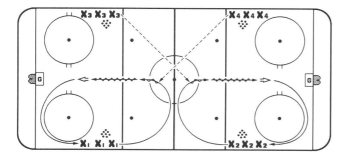

PS 33

X1 and X2 cut through the center circle, receiving a diagonal pass from X3 and X4. After the shot, X3 and X4 skate the oval, receiving a diagonal pass from X1 and X2. Change sides halfway through drill to take forehand and backhand passes.

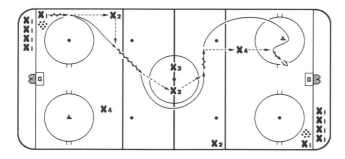

PS 34

X1 passes to X2 at the blue line and X2 returns the pass as X1 reaches the blue line. X1 then gives a pass to X3, skates the outside of the circle, and takes a return pass from X3. X1 then passes to X4, drives wide and deep, and takes a return pass from X4 for a shot on goal.

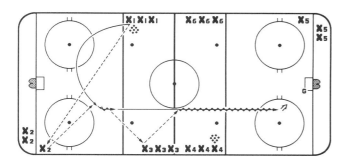

PS 35

X1 passes to X2. X1 curls deep for a return pass from X1 and does a give-and-go with X3, then shoots on goal. Use both ends at the same time.

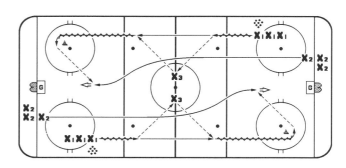

PS 36

X1 is by the boards at the top of the circle with X2 positioned at the bottom of the circle. X1 and X2 start at the same time, X2 at the blue line passes to X3 at center, picks up speed, gets a return pass, skates to the pylon, and passes to the trailer X2 in the slot. Use both sides of the ice.

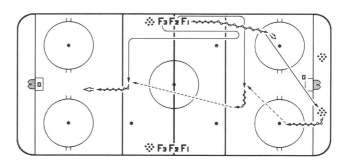

PS 37

F1 takes a shot on goal, picks up a puck, and passes to a curling F2. F2 skates over the blue line and passes to a breaking F3, who has read the play and moved into position for a fast break on goal.

Variation: Have a coach in the corner pass the puck to F1.

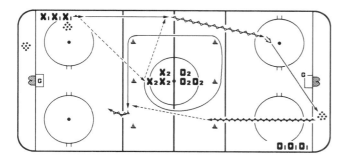

PS 38

X1 does the give-and-go pass with X2. After shooting, X1 picks up a puck and races to the blue line to make a pass to X2, who skated around the perimeter of the pylons after the initial pass to X1. The drill can be performed on both sides at the same time.

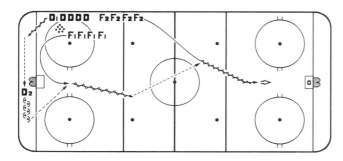

PS 39

D1 on the hash marks skates below the goal line and passes to D2. D2 skates backward and makes a quick pass to the curling F1. F1 skates to the blueline and passes to F2 who skated up ice on the whistle that started the drill.

Variation: F1 follows for a two-on-zero.

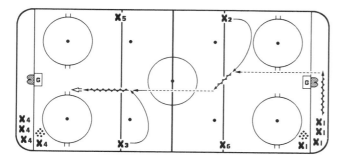

PS 40

Group X1, X2, and X3 and group X4, X5, and X6 go at the same time. X1 carries the puck behind the net and passes to X2 and replaces X2 at that position.

X2 skates through the neutral zone and passes to a curling X3 and replaces X3 at that position. X3 skates in and takes a shot on goal and goes to the X4 line.

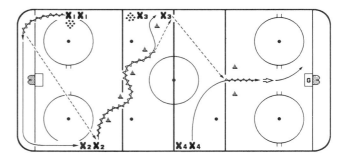

PS 41

This drill combines puckhandling and passing. Divide the players as shown. X1 skates with a puck, waiting for X2 to call for the puck, at which time X1 passes to X2. X2 carries the puck through the cones to the X3 line. X3 waits for X4 to call for the puck, at which time he passes to X4. After shooting, X4 skates back along the boards to join the X1 line. Also, changing the location of X1 or X3 (particularly X3) will change pass receiver X2 or X4 results.

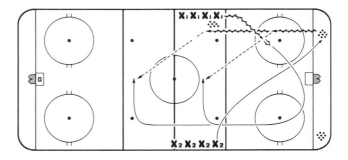

PS 42

X1 and X2 start. X1 shoots on goal. X2 watches for rebounds and then skates to the corner to retrieve a puck. X2 breaks up-ice and can pass to X1, who can be in one of two positions to receive the pass. The first position is just outside the blue line and the second position is on the other side of center. If stretching, watch for off-sides.

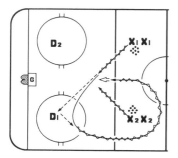

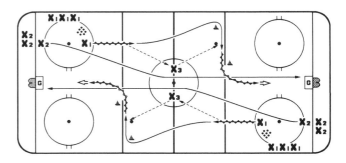

PS 43

Place the players as shown. X1 does a give-and-go pass with D1, receives a return pass, skates full speed into the neutral zone and around the back of the line on that side before going in on goal for a shot. X2 repeats on the other side.

PS 46

X1 and X2 start at the same time. X1 starts at the top of the circle and X2 at the bottom of the circle. X1 makes a pass to X3 at the center-ice circle and sprints for the far blue line. X1 skates around the pylon, cuts in, and takes a return pass from X3 being sure to stay on-side. After receiving the pass, X1 drives for the net and takes a shot on goal or drops a pass for the trailing X2 or skates wide with the puck to pass to X2 in the slot.

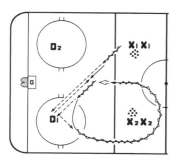

PS 44

The same as the previous drill except X1 does touch-passing (twice) with D1 before cutting through the top of the circle.

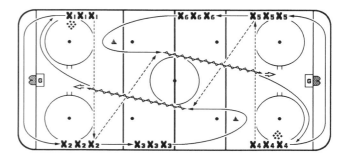

PS 47

Both ends go at the same time, with X1 and X4 starting the drill. X1 passes to X2 (X1 skates behind the net to X2 line). X2 passes to the curling X6 from the other side (X2 moves to X3 line). X6 takes a shot on goal and goes to the X4 line.

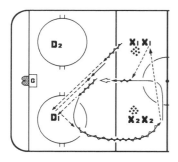

PS 45

The same as the previous drill, except this time when X1 skates around the other line, he gives a pass to the last player in the line, receives it back, and then goes in for a shot on goal.

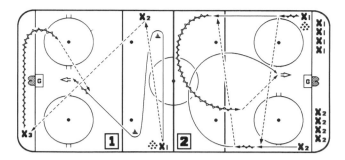

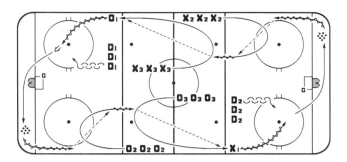

PS 48

(1) X1 passes to X2 and X2 passes to X3. X3 skates behind the net and passes to the slot to X1 who has skated laterally across the ice and around the pylons. After the first pass, X1 takes a shot on goal. X1 goes to X3, X3 to X2, and X2 to X1.

(2) X1 and X2 pass wide and swing into the neutral zone for a two-on-zero.

PS 50

X1 and X2 start the drill with pucks by taking a shot on goal. X1 picks up a puck in the corner and passes to X2 (facing the puck) with X1 going to the X2 line. X2 curls and passes to X3, who has skated inside/out to the boards to receive a pass from X2 with X2 going to the X3 line. X3 takes a shot on goal, picks up a puck in the corner, and passes to O2 to keep the drill moving. D1 and D2 skate backward and then turn to check the shooter after the pass has been received.

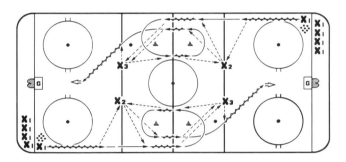

PS 49

X1 passes to X2 and skates up the boards for a return pass. X1 skates over the center red line and passes to X3, does a tight turn around the pylon, and takes a return pass from X3. X1 then passes to X2 again, does a tight turn around the pylon, and heads up-ice again. As X1 crosses center again, a pass is made to X3 again and then X1 skates down the boards for a return pass from X3 before going in on goal for a shot. Use both sides of the rink at the same time.

8
Shooting

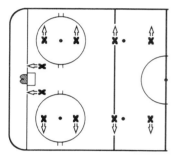

SH I

The players shoot from a stationary position at the boards. They shoot 10 high shots, 10 low shots, and then alternate between high and low shots. Mark some spots on the boards (low and high) and have the players shoot for the marks. Use half or full ice. Use different types of shots.

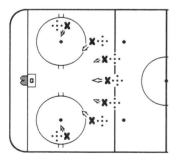

SH 2

The players are stationary in a semi-circle starting from the blue-line hash marks. The players shoot in rapid succession. After each player has had a shot, they move in five feet closer and use wrist shots only.

Variation: Shoot alternate rather than in succession – left side, right side, next left, etc.

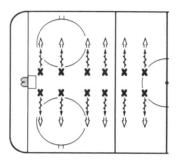

SH 3

The players shoot against the boards from a moving position with the players working from the center. Use half or full ice. Use different types of shots.

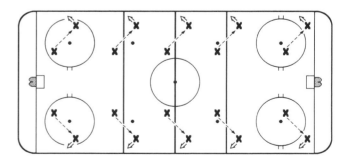

SH 4

Put the players in pairs. The middle player shoots along the ice towards the boards and the player near the boards tips the puck in the direction they want. Change positions every 10 shots.

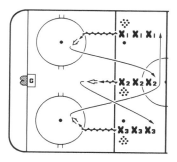

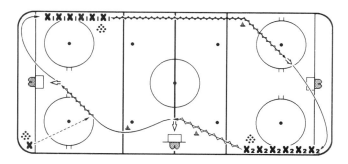

SH 5

Players shoot from all three positions. Player X1 shoots first and then goes to line X2. Players rotate through all three positions.

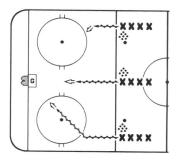

SH 6

Three lines start simultaneously. Line one shoots from the top of the circle, line two from the high slot, and line three from the bottom of the circle. Alternate lines and have long shots come from both sides.

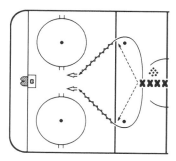

SH 7

The player receives a pass from the center, cuts in and shoots from the wing and returns to center. The next player swings to the opposite side and receives a pass from the next player in the line.

SH 8

Use three goaltenders for this drill. Both lanes start at the same time. X1 skates down the ice at full speed and shoots a slap shot on goal before the top of the circle. X2 takes a backhand shot on the goaltender at center ice and skates into the other zone, receives a pass, and takes a wrist shot.

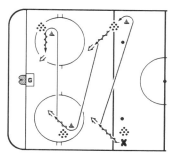

SH 9

The players are positioned as shown. X shoots from the blue line, skates across-ice around a pylon, picks up a puck, then shoots again. X then skates across-ice again, around a pylon, picks up a puck, and shoots again. X skates across the ice one more time, around a pylon, and picks up a puck for the final shot on goal. Have different types of shots at each location.

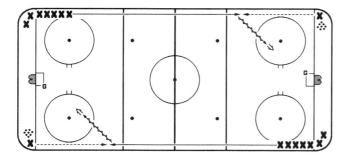

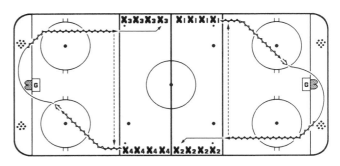

SH 10

The players from the corner skate the length of the ice, receive a pass from the corner, and shoot while in stride. The players then join the line in their end of the rink. Players start five seconds apart.

SH 13

The players X1 and X4 start the drill simultaneously and take shots on goal. Players X2 and X3 start when X1 and X4 shoot. After X1 and X4 shoot, they go behind the net to the opposite corner, pick up a puck, and skate towards the blue line. They now make a lateral pass across the ice to the next player in the line.

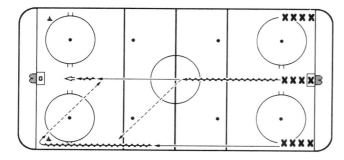

SH 11

Two players pass to each other with the board-side (outside) player passing to the slot after skating past the pylon. Alternate sides and players.

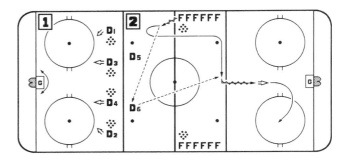

SH 14

(1) Point Shooting. Have defencemen shoot from inside the blue line.
(2) Mid-lane Shooting. Drill starts with F passing to D. F then skates up-ice (use pylon or dot), cutting laterally to the middle to receive a pass from D. Forwards switch sides after the shot so as to receive passes on the forehand and backhand.

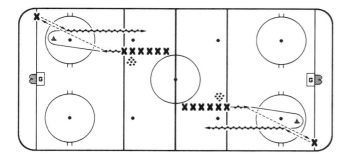

SH 12

The players at the blue line pass to X in the corner and then skate around the pylon to receive a return pass. The puck carrier then skates to the end of the ice for a shot on goal.

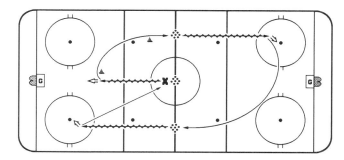

SH 15

Place three sets of pucks as shown. X starts from the middle and takes a shot on goal. X then goes back to the neutral zone to get another puck and shoots on goal at the other end of the ice. X returns to the neutral zone for another puck and takes a final shot on goal before returning to the line in the center-ice circle.

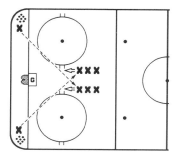

SH 16

The players are stationary in the slot and shoot as soon as the puck is passed out. Alternate sides.

Variation: Pass from one corner and shoot. Pass from the other corner and shoot.

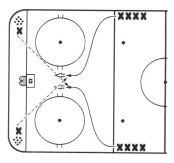

SH 17

After shooting the puck, the player goes to the corner from where the pass came. The player passing the puck then goes to the end of the line on the same side of the rink.

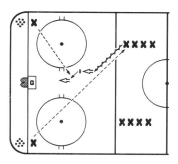

SH 18

The variation of the previous drill. After the player has taken the first shot, the player stops in the high slot, receives a second pass from the opposite corner, and then shoots again.

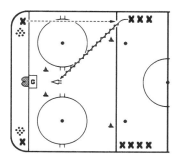

SH 19

The players receive a pass early from the corner and the players cut around a pylon and shoot from their backhand side of the slot area.

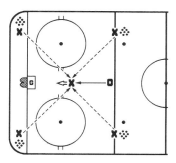

SH 20

Pucks are passed to the shooter in the middle from different players and from different angles with the last pass being chased by a checker. Rotate positions.

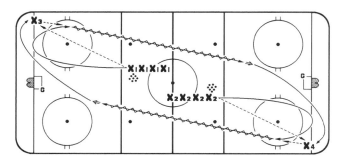

SH 21

A player receives a pass from the opposite corner and shoots on the net. A player from the opposite side drives to the net looking for a rebound. Alternate sides with the pass outs.

SH 24

Players X1 and X2 pass to their partners in the corners. X1 and X2 skate into the corners, turn up the ice, receive a return pass, and skate the length of the ice for a shot on goal. X1 and X2 then go to the opposite corner to become the passers.

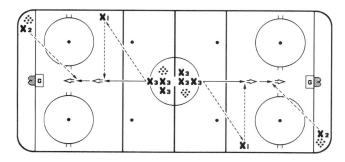

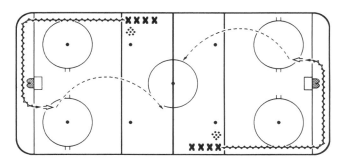

SH 22

X1 and X2 are in stationary positions. All the other players are in the center-ice circle. X3 passes to X1 for the give-and-shoot. X3 receives a second puck from X2 for a second shot.

SH 25

The players skate in and around the net and try to flip shot the puck in the air so it will land out in the neutral zone or in the offensive zone without going over the goal line for icing. Practice forehand and backhand clearing the zone shots.

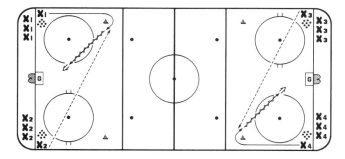

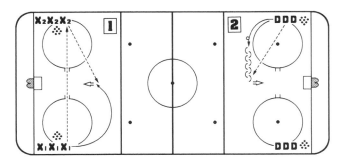

SH 23

Player X1 skates around the pylon and receives a pass from X2 and then shoots on goal. After X2 makes the pass, X2 skates around the pylon and receives a pass from X1. Groups X3 and X4 do the same drill.

SH 26

(1) Forwards: X1 passes across the ice to X2. X1 cuts for the high slot for a return pass from X2 and takes a one-timer shot. Now, X2 passes to X1, etc.
(2) Defence: D skates across the top of the circle, pivots backward, receives a pass from the boards, and takes a shot on goal.

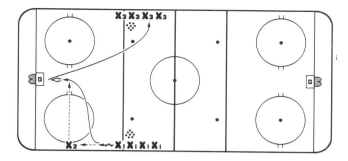

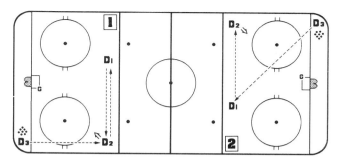

SH 27

X1 passes to X2 on the hash marks. X1 drives to the net for the return pass and tries to one-time the shot from the slot.

SH 30

(1) D3 in the corner passes to D2 who passes to D1. D1 returns the pass to D2, who shoots on goal.
(2) D3 passes to D1, who passes to D2, who then shoots on goal. Use both sides of the ice.

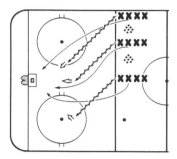

SH 28

The forward and rebounder start from the first line. The shooter shoots from the top of the far circle and the rebounder drives for the net. The forward from the second line skates in and shoots from in close. The rebounder follows and drives for the net. The forward from the third line shoots from the near face-off dot and the rebounder drives for the net.

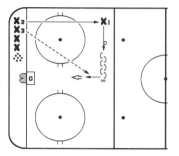

SH 31

On the whistle, X1 and X2 start the drill. X1 skates towards the middle, pivots, skating backward waiting for a pass from X3 for a shot on goal. X2, who went to the position of X1, receives a pass from X3. X1 passes to X2 for the second shot. The shooter goes to the opposite corner.

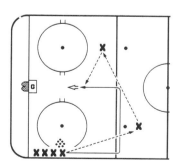

SH 29

The player skates from the corner, passes to one player who passes to the other stationary player, and then a return pass is made to the forward.

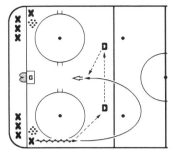

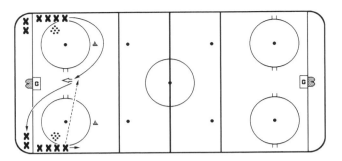

SH 32

The player skates from the corner and passes to the nearest defenceman. The defenceman passes to the other defenceman and then back to the forward. The forward then goes in and shoots on the goaltender and then moves to the other corner. The defencemen stay in the same positions for this drill.

SH 35

A player comes out from the corner, around the top of the circle, and receives a pass from the opposite side for a shot on goal. The passer then becomes the shooter from the other side.

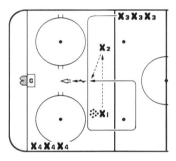

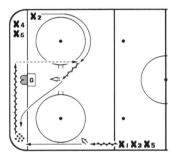

SH 33

The pass goes from X1 to X2, then to X3, who takes a shot on the goaltender and goes to the line in the corner. X1 goes to the position of X2 and X2 goes to the shooting line.

SH 36

X1 takes a shot on goal, then skates to the corner to retrieve a puck at which time X2 starts to skate around the top of the circle and down the slot. X1 in the meantime skates behind the net and passes to X2 in the slot for a shot on goal. X1 joins the other line. X2 after shooting picks up a puck and passes to X3 to repeat the drill. X2 joins the line at the blue line.

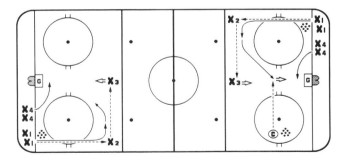

SH 34

X1 passes to X2 and follows the pass. X2 quickly passes to X3 for a shot on goal. X4 slips to the side of the net for a possible tip in, rebound, or deflection. The coach then passes another puck to X1 for another shot.

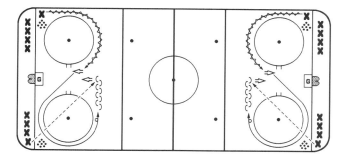

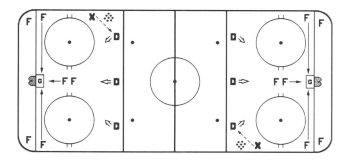

SH 37

A player carries the puck around the top of the circle and shoots from the slot. The player continues to skate in and around the bottom of the far circle, pivoting backward at the top of the circle and receiving a pass from the corner for another shot on goal.

Variation: The player can stop after the second shot, move to the high slot, receive another pass from the corner and shoot.

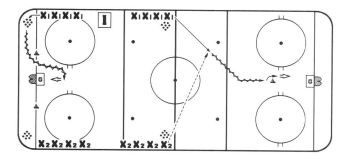

SH 38

(1) A player skates out from the corner between the pylon and the post for a shot on goal. Use both sides.
(2) Forehand/Backhand Shooting: A player receives a pass and skates towards the pylon. The body is on one side of the pylon but the shot is from the other side. Use forehand and backhand shots. Change sides after four shots each.

SH 39

Two forwards stand in front of the net and try to screen the goaltender and deflect shots from the three defencemen on the points. The defencemen shoot three shots each and then rotate.

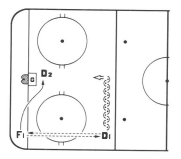

SH 40

DI starts the drill by passing to FI. FI then passes to DI and goes to the front of the goal. D2 skates backward to the middle and shoots while in motion. FI tries for a deflection, screen, rebound, etc.

Variation: Add D2 to cover FI.

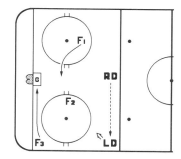

SH 41

The puck is at the left point. FI moves to the front of the goal, F3 positions off the post beside the goal, and F2 covers the high slot. D shoots. All forwards try for deflections, rebounds, etc.

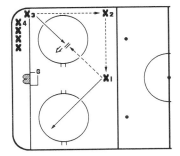

SH 42

X3 passes to X2, who passes quickly to X1 in the middle. X1 touch-passes the puck to X3, who has moved to the face-off dot area for a one-time shot on goal. X3 goes to X2, X2 to X1, and X1 goes to the opposite corner.

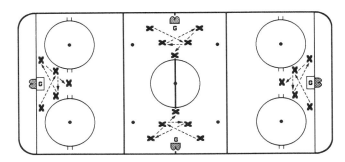

SH 43

Have five players in front of each goal and touch-pass the puck to all players. The last player takes a quick shot on goal.

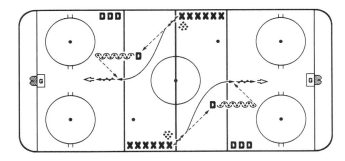

SH 44

X passes to D on the face-off dot. D skates backward (with the puck) to the top of the circle. D then passes back to X, who goes in for a shot on goal.

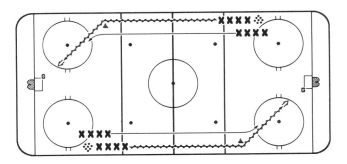

SH 45

The puck carrier starts at the blue line and the checker stands slightly behind. The checker tries to apply pressure before the puck carrier shoots after skating past the pylon. Use both sides of the ice.

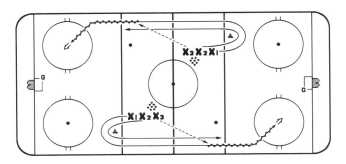

SH 46

X2 chases X1, applying pressure. X3 passes to X1 and X1 tries to shoot with X2 in chase.

Variation: Add another player for a give-and-go.

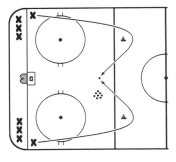

SH 47

Race for the puck and shoot. Players must start at the same time, race around the pylons with the first player taking the puck and shooting on the goal-tender. The trailing player tries to check the puck carrier.

Variation: Skate backward to the cones, pivot and race for the puck.

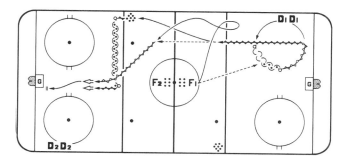

SH 48

FI starts the drill by passing to DI at the top of the circle. DI skates backward to the bottom of the circle, then heads up ice. FI, after passing, curls inside out by the boards and heads up-ice to receive a pass from DI. DI, after passing, skates to the blue line, retrieves a puck, skates backward to the middle of the ice, and shoots on goal. FI gets any rebound or tip-in opportunity.

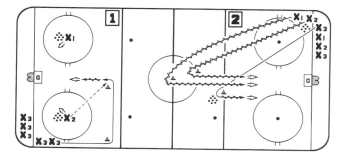

SH 49

(1) XI shoots, X2 shoots and then passes to X3, who is skating a pattern. X3 shoots. X3 moves to XI, XI moves to X2, and X2 joins the skating line.
(2) Position players XI, X2, and X3 and take shots on goal.

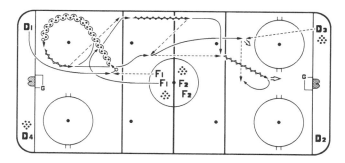

SH 50

Place defencemen in corners and forwards in the center-ice circle. FI passes to DI, DI receives puck

and skates backward around the circle and passes to FI, who has curled to the boards. FI back-passes to DI, drives to the blue line, and cuts across to receive the puck for DI. DI passes and moves up over the blue line for a pass from D3 and shot on goal.

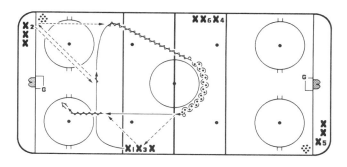

SH 51

XI skates across the ice, receiving and giving a pass to X2 in the corner. X2 passes back to XI, who skates to the middle of the ice, skating backward around the circle and at the red line passing to X3 for another give-and-go. XI takes a shot on goal. X4 starts when XI crosses the center red line.

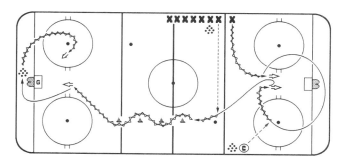

SH 52

The players drive to the net, shoot, skate around the net, receive a pass from the coach, shoot, skate up the ice, and receive a pass from the starting line. X then skates through the pylons, shoots on goal, picks up a puck behind the net, and comes out front for a final shot.

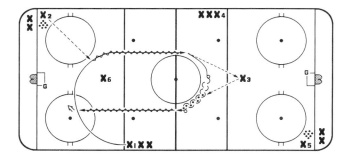

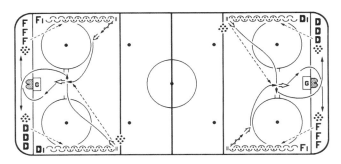

SH 53

Place X3 and X6 in position. X1 starts the wide swing and receives a pass from X2 in the corner. X1 skates to center, passes to X3 for the give-and-receive while agility-skating. X1 then shoots on goal. X4 starts when X1 gets over the center red line.

SH 55

D1 and F2 receive a pass from the corner as they skate backward to the blue line. D1 shoots from the blue line. F1 skates forward to the top of the circle and shoots. D1 passes another puck to F1 in the slot for another shot. Rotate players on both sides.

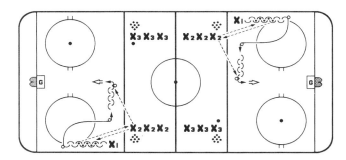

SH 54

X1 skates backward and receives a pass from X2. X1, after reaching the hash marks, passes back to X2. X1 skates towards the blue line, pivots, and skates laterally backward to the middle of the ice, where X2 feeds another pass to X1 for a shot on goal.

9
Checking

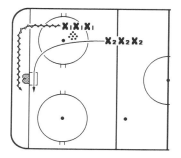

CH 1

X1 is the puck carrier and skates behind the net without stopping. The checker X2 tries to angle X1 into the boards or corner.

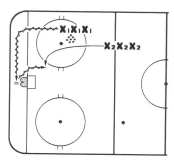

CH 2

X1 carries the puck behind the goal and stops. X2 stops in front of the goal. As X1 comes out from behind the goal (left or right side), X2 tries to check X1 off the puck. The players then switch positions.

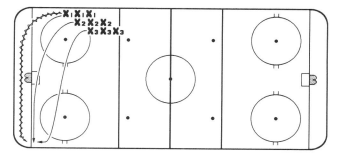

CH 3

X1 carries the puck behind the net. X2 forechecks and angles X1 to the boards with a bodycheck. X3 retrieves the puck and takes a shot on goal.

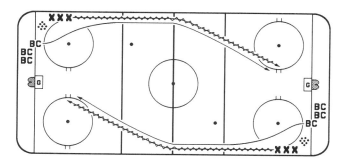

CH 4

X starts on the board-side hash marks or face-off dot. BC starts from the bottom of the circle. On the whistle, both players head for the opposite end of the ice. X tries to get a shot on goal while the BC tries to prevent the shot from being taken.

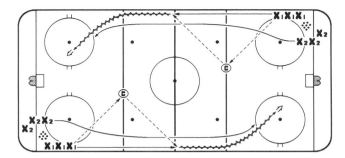

CH 5

X1 passes to the coach for the give-and-go play. The coach passes back to X1. X2 backchecks. The players reverse roles coming back on the opposite side.

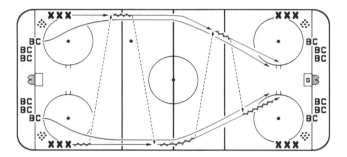

CH 6

Two X players try to pass the puck back and forth to each other before taking a shot on goal while two BCs try to apply pressure and intercept passes. The two BCs skate to the net.

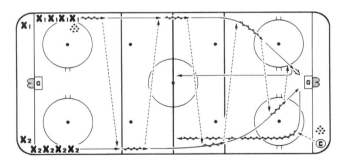

CH 7

The players skate the length of the ice wide-passing with a shot on goal at the far end. One of the players receives a pass from the corner and the other player becomes a backchecker or plays defence.

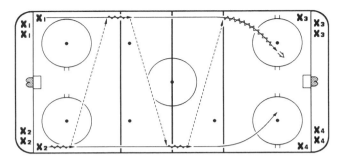

CH 8

X1 and X2 attack two-on-zero. On the whistle, X3 and X4 break out two-on-zero but X1 and X2 must now backcheck on X3 and X4.

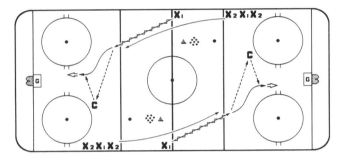

CH 9

Position the players as shown. X1 and X2 start at the same time. As X1 comes into the zone, the coach has his stick on the ice or in the air. If the stick is on the ice, X1 passes to the coach, who returns the pass to X1 who takes a shot on goal. If the coach's stick is off the ice, X1 goes in and shoots. X2 applies pressure to X1 going down the ice.

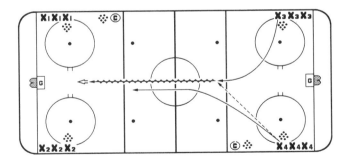

CH 10

X4 passes to X3 and then backchecks, trying to catch X3 before a shot on goal can be taken.

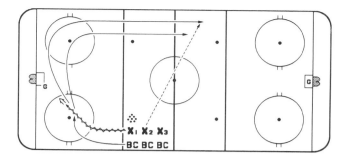

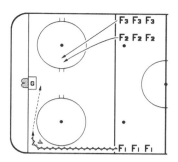

CH 11

X1 takes a shot on goal and curls towards the circle (below the face-off dot) at half-speed. BC starts after X1 shoots and tries to stay between X1 and X2 to stop any passes. X1 breaks hard from the blue line out while trying to receive the pass from X2.

CH 14

F1 carries the puck wide and deep and tries to pass to F3. F2 backchecks F3 to the goal and tries to prevent F3 from touching the puck.

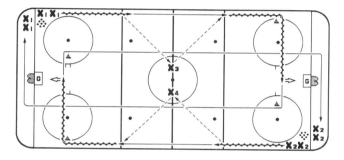

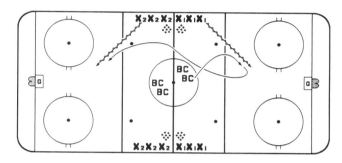

CH 12

X1 and X2 start at the same time. X1 does a give-and-go pass with X3 at center ice, receives the puck back, skates around the pylon, and takes a shot on goal. As soon as X1 shoots, X2 starts by passing to X4. X1 tries to backcheck X2. Rotate the two players in the middle.

CH 15

X1 drives towards the goal. The backchecker (BC) at the center red line backchecks. As soon as X1 shoots, BC must try to catch X2 going in the opposite direction. Even if BC can't catch the player, BC must still skate hard to the net.

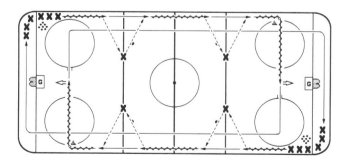

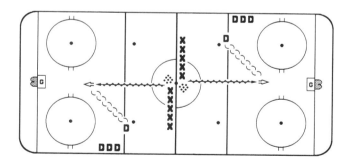

CH 13

This is similar to the previous drill but this time the players do a double give-and-go play with the players on the blue lines. The players must shoot from the slot.

CH 16

X starts on the center face-off dot and D stands on the neutral-zone dot. Both start at the same time with D trying to stop X from scoring.

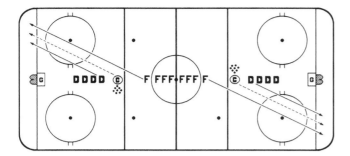

CH 17

The coach shoots the puck into the corner. Players D and F go after the puck. D tries to get the puck to carry it to the blue line rather than shoot it out. F tries to get the puck for a shot on goal.

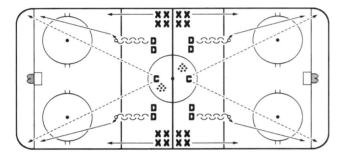

CH 18

D starts between the blue line and the forechecker X by the boards on the center red line. D skates backward to the blue line as the coach shoots a puck into the corner. D pivots at the blue line and goes after the puck. X tries to get the puck from D.

Variation: Use two forecheckers.

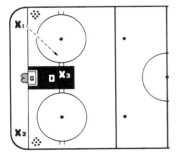

CH 19

X1 and X2 take turns trying to get the puck to X in the slot. X3 can move anywhere in the shaded area. D must try to stop X3 from getting a scoring opportunity.

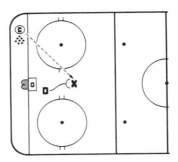

CH 20

The coach passes to X for a shot on goal. D tries to force the shooter to his backhand side.

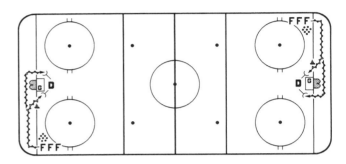

CH 21

F comes out of the corner and tries to beat D and the goaltender by putting the puck in the far or short side. F must go between the pylon and the net on the short side.

Variation: Use 2 Ds, one at each post in front of the net. F tries to come out in front from either side.

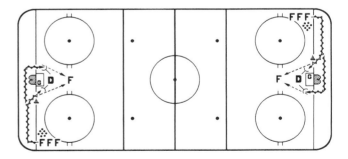

CH 22

This is the same as the previous drill but the puck carrier has the option of passing to the forward in the high slot.

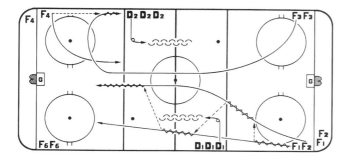

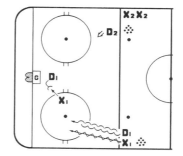

CH 23

This drill is a two-on-one with a backchecker. F1 and F2 go two-on-one against D1. F3 comes out of the opposite corner as the backchecker. After the play is made, F3 curls to F4 or F6 (in this case F4), receives a pass from F4, and goes two-on-one with D2. The opposite corner F6 becomes the backchecker. Forwards who are waiting in the corner must read the direction of the backchecker and react accordingly.

to the goal as D1 is receiving the puck. D2 tries to stop X2 from getting the rebound or getting to the goal.

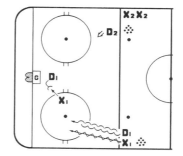

CH 26

D1 plays X1 one-on-one from the board side. After X1 shoots, X1 tries for position in front of the goal. X1 tries to move out so the goaltender can see the shot coming from D2. After the shot from D2, D2 plays X2 one-on-one.

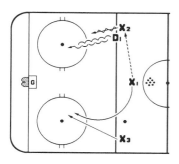

CH 24

X1 passes to X2 and then backchecks X3 on the opposite side. D1 plays X2 one-on-one. X1 has the option to pass to X2 or try to beat D1. X3 drives to the net.

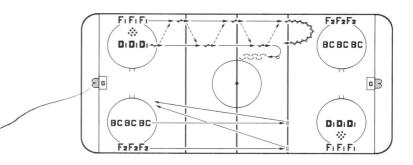

CH 27

Four players start at the same time, heading for the opposite blue line. F2 and BC skate with BC maintaining an inside position at all times. F1 and D1 pass to each other, but at the opposite blue line the drill becomes a one-on-one for F1 with D1. F1 can try to pass to F2 if the backchecker allows it.

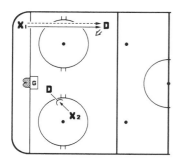

CH 25

X1 passes to D1 and rushes to D1 to force D1 to shoot quickly. X2 starts in the circle and tries to get

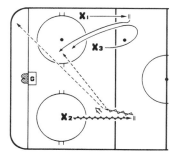

CH 28

All three X players start at the same time. X1 and X2 with a puck skate outside the blue line, stop, and then re-enter the zone, driving for the net. X3 skates to the blue line, reads X1, and backchecks on X1 coming back into the zone. X2 tries to get the puck to X1 by a dump-in, pass, or shot on goal.

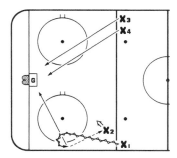

CH 29

X1 brings the puck into the zone and delays at the hash marks. X4 backchecks against X3, who is trying to drive to the net. X1 can pass to X3 if free of the backchecker or pass back to the point to X2, who shoots on goal.

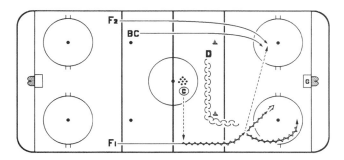

CH 30

All four players start at the same time but F1 and F2 must stay in the outside lanes until they reach the blue line. D starts at the pylon and skates laterally

backward around the next pylon for a one-on-one. F1 can shoot, pass, or try to beat the D one-on-one.

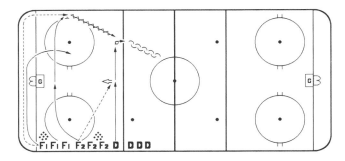

CH 31

D skates to the middle lane, receives a pass from F2 for a shot on goal. After passing the puck, F2 drives for the goal for a rebound or a deflection. After the shot, F1 shoots a puck around the boards for F2, who goes one-on-one with D. F1 follows the pass around and becomes the backchecker.

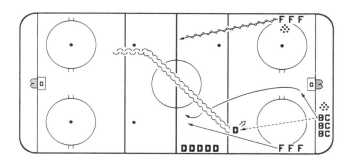

CH 32

To start the drill, BC on the goal line passes to D at the top of the circle for a shot on goal. BC skates to the side of the net after the pass to D for a possible deflection. On the whistle, F1 and F2 break out two-on-one with D1 and BC.

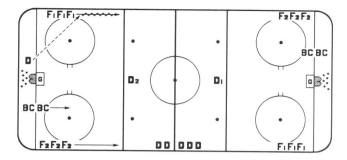

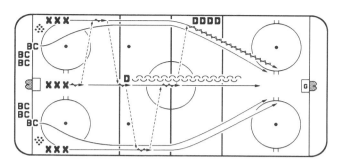

CH 33

D starts the drill from behind the goal by passing to F1 or F2. The backchecker takes the player without the puck. F1 and F2 attack D2 for a two-on-one with a backchecker. After the play is over, the defending D2 or BC retrieves a puck from behind the goal and starts the next group.

CH 36

Three forwards try to pass to each other coming down the ice. The one D must read the two backcheckers' position.

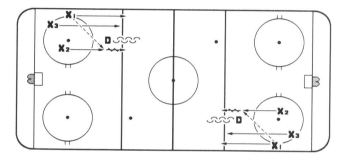

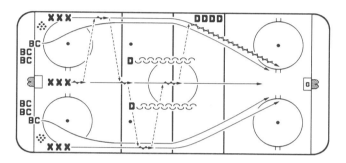

CH 34

X1 passes to X2 for a two-on-one with D. X3 backchecks X1. D reads the play and plays X2 one-on-one if X1 is in check.

CH 37

This is similar to the previous drill but if the wingers are covered, then two D can force the play at the blue line.

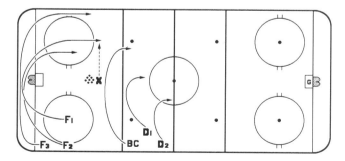

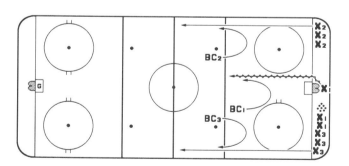

CH 35

Set up players as shown. The three forwards start by skating behind the net and turn up the ice. X passes to F2 coming out of the zone. The three forwards attack the two D and one BC. All three defenders start when the forwards go behind the net.

CH 38

BC2 and BC3 pick up forwards X2 and X3 as they come out of the zone. BC1 picks up X1, who has a puck, and tries to force X1 to move the puck or shoot it in.

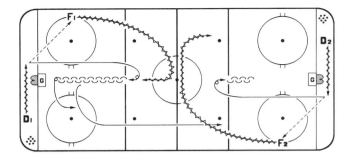

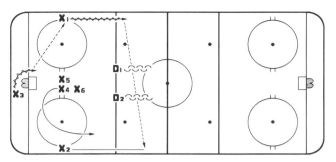

CH 39

D1 skates behind the goal, passes to F1 and F1 goes outside the blue line and comes back one-on-one against D1. After this play is finished, the coach blows the whistle and a one-on-one starts at the other end with D2 and F2. F1 then skates to the end and joins F2 for a two-on-one. D1 backchecks and picks up F2.

CH 41

X1, X2, and X3 break out three-on-two on D1 and D2. The coach predetermines with X4, X5, or X6 if there will be one or two backcheckers or a trailing backchecker. D1 and D2 must read the rush and react to the situation.

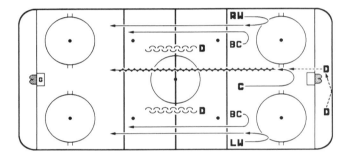

CH 40

The drill starts with a D-to-D pass, a pass to a forward and a five-on-four breakout. The two backcheckers pick up the lanes, allow the D to stand up at the blue line, and concentrate on the puck carrier. When the initial rush is completed, a five-on-two starts the opposite way.

Variation: Use one backchecker and one forechecker.

10
One-, Two-, and Three-on-Zero

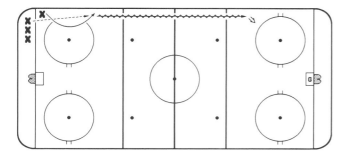

1/0 1

The first player curls as shown, receives a pass from the second player, skates the length of the ice, and shoots.

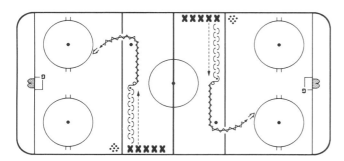

1/0 2

The first player skates backward from the boards, receives a pass from the second player, pivots, skates around the far dot, and shoots.

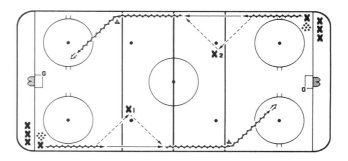

1/0 3

The players pass to a stationary player on the face-off dot and receive a return pass. The player with the puck skates wide to the far blue line then drives for the goal for a shot.

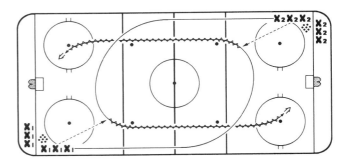

1/0 4

The Horseshoe Drill. Players start at each end and skate inside the far blue line, receive a pass, skate down the ice, and shoot.

Variations:

(1) Players passing, X2 receives a drop pass from X1 and returns the pass to X1.

(2) Players passing, X2 follows X1 for a possible rebound and then curls and receives a pass from the corner.

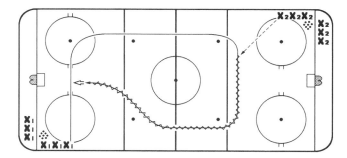

1/0 5

The Reverse Horseshoe Drill. This is the same as the Horseshoe Drill but players skate the pattern opposite to the previous drill.

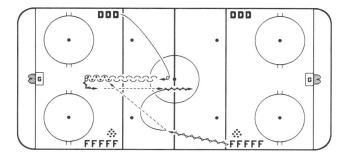

1/0 6

D1 skates through the face-off circle and then F1 starts. D1 pivots then skates backward with F1 passing to D1. D1 steps up and returns the pass to F1. D1 skates to the center red line, stops, skates backward to the top of the circle, pivots, goes to the corner, and returns to the D line. F1 shoots at the other end and returns to the F line.

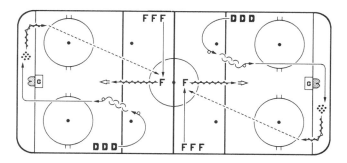

1/0 7

D skates around the face-off dot, pivots, skates backward to the top of the circle, pivots again, and skates full speed to pick up a puck. After retrieving the puck, D makes a long breakout pass to F, skating

through the center-ice circle. F starts after D picks up the puck. F takes a shot on goal. Both players go back to their original positions.

Variation: This drill can be used as a one-on-one. D can skate forward and then backward to take the forward receiving the pass.

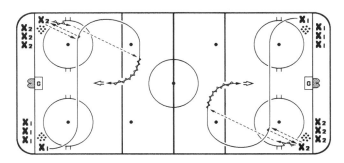

1/0 8

X1 comes out of the corner and receives a pass from X2. X1 returns the pass, circles high, and receives a second pass from X2. X1 then moves in and shoots on goal.

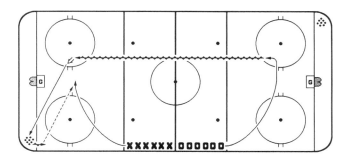

1/0 9

To start the drill, two players start from the side boards at opposite blue lines, loop in as shown, and receive a pass from the corners from the coaches. They then skate the length of the ice, shoot on goal, retrieve a puck in the corner, and pass to the next player coming off the boards.

Variation: Two-on-none and three-on-none. Only one group of two or three goes at one time, shoots, retrieves a puck, and then starts the next group, who loop in above the face-off circle.

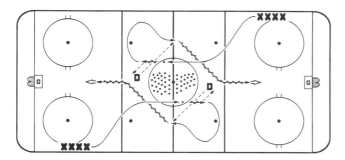

1/0 10

After picking up a puck in the center-ice circle, player X passes to D, curls outside, receives a return pass from D, and goes one-on-zero on the goaltender.

Variation: D follows the play in as a trailer for a two-on-none.

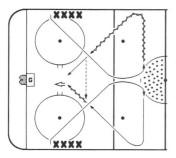

2/0 11

One player from each side starts at the same time. They skate to the center-ice circle and one player picks up a puck. Both players then go wide to the boards and drive for the net. The puck carrier can shoot on goal or pass it to the other player for a shot on goal.

Variation: Start the drill with a one-on-zero.

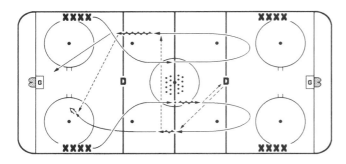

2/0 12

This drill is similar to the previous drill but D can now pass to either forward for the two-on-zero. The forwards can pass to each other and have one shooting and the other driving to the goal.

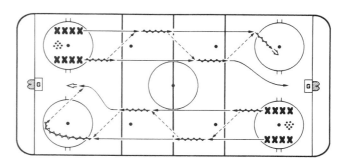

2/0 13

The players on the left side pass to each other with the board-side player shooting and the middle-lane player going for the rebound. On the other side, the board-side player goes wide and passes the slot for a one-timer.

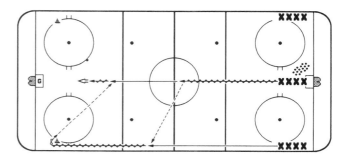

2/0 14

The players from two of the lanes pass to each other with the board-side (outside) player passing to the slot when at the hash marks or pylons. Alternate sides and players.

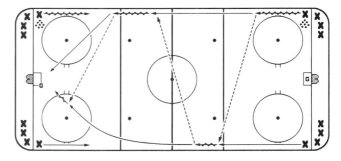

2/0 15

The players make long, wide passes going down the ice two-on-zero. When one group finishes, the next group starts.

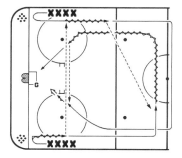

2/0 16

The players skate from both corners, passing the puck wide to each other, curl in the neutral zone, and attack two-on-zero.

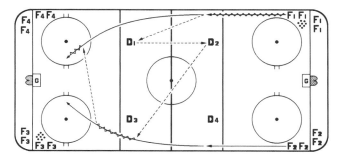

2/0 17

F1 and F2 skate down the ice. F1 passes to D1, D1 to D2, and D2 passes to a wide-breaking F2 for a two-on-zero with F1. F3 and F4 go in the opposite direction.

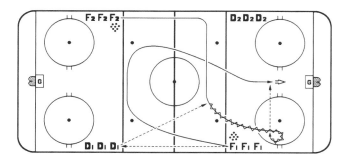

2/0 18

F1 and F2 start the drill at the same time. F2 skates up-ice and then laterally across the ice taking a pass from D1. F2 then skates wide and deep to the hash marks, does a delay to buy time, and then passes to F1 for a shot on goal. F1 had skated to the far blue line, laterally across the ice, then drives for the slot area to receive the pass from F2 and then shoots on goal.

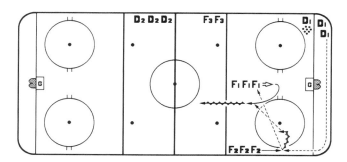

2/0 19

D1 shoots the puck around the boards. F2 reads the play, steps in, picks up the puck, and passes to F1, who goes one-on-none for a shot on goal. The second option is for F2 to pick up the puck, pass to F1, and go two-on-none for a shot on goal.

Variation: F2 dumps the puck back into the corner to F1, who went there. F2 drives to the net waiting for a pass from F1 and a shot on goal.

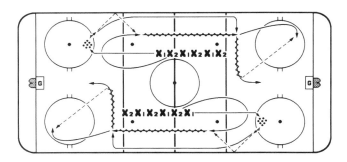

2/0 20

Two players in each line skate forward. The first player picks up a puck in the top of the circle and passes (or board-passes) to the second player, who reads the play and curls to the boards to receive the pass. A two-on-none results with the puck carrier shooting, dropping a pass, delaying to the boards, etc.

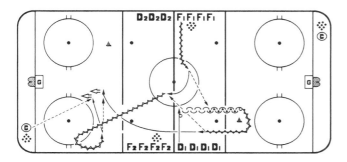

2/0 21

D1 and F1 start at the same time. D1 skates towards the center-ice circle, pivots, skates backward, and receives a pass from F1. D1 skates around the pylon and returns the pass to F1. F1 drives to the goal for a shot. D1 follows up to the blue line, receives a pass from the corner, and takes a shot on goal. F1 tries for a rebound or a deflection.

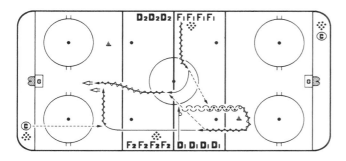

2/0 22

This is the same as the previous drill but F1 carries the puck, does a delay, and passes to D coming into the zone as the trailer.

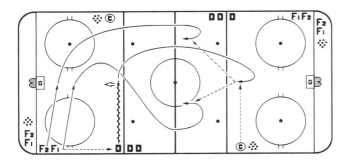

2/0 23

F1 passes to D1. D1 comes across the blue line and shoots. F1 and F2 go to the net to deflect. D skates to the far blue line and takes a pass from the coach. F1 and F2 skate to the far blue line and receive a pass from D1 and go two-on-zero.

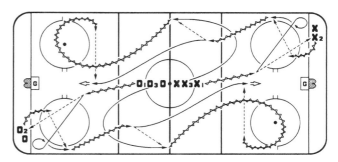

3/0 24

X1 passes in the corner to X2. X1 skates to the boards and gets into a breakout position to receive a return pass from X2. X3 reads the breakout and curls to the outside to receive a pass from X1. X3 carries the puck into the offensive zone and does a curl (delay), passing to the oncoming X1.

Variation: X2 skates out to play O1 and O3 for a two-on-one.

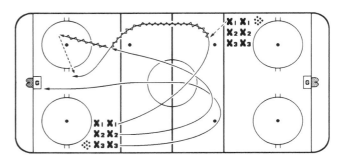

3/0 25

All three X players of a line start together. They swing through the neutral zone as shown, with X1 taking a pass from the opposite side. X1 skates into the zone and cuts to the middle, dropping a pass for X2 going wide. X2 goes wide and deep and passes to X1 in the slot for a shot on goal. X2 drives to the net from the neutral zone. Players switch position in their line until they have skated all three positions.

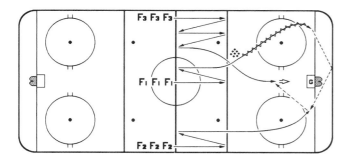 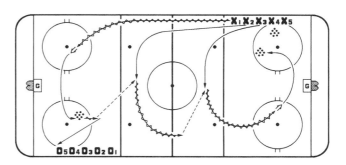

3/0 26

All three forwards start at the same time. F1 skates to the blue line and back to the center red line before proceeding into the zone. F1 picks up a puck at the blue line and goes wide and deep. F2 skates to the blue line and back before driving for the net. F3 skates to the blue line and back twice before skating for the slot. F1 board-passes to F2, who passes to F3 in the slot for a shot on goal.

3/0 27

X1 starts the drill by skating down the ice and shooting on goal. X1 picks up a puck and passes to X2. X2 skates up-ice as X1 shoots, getting into position to receive the pass. X3 skates up-ice, cutting across the ice as X2 receives the first pass. X2 passes to X3. X3 drives to the net, X2 follows. After the shot, X3 passes another puck to X1 to start a new group.

11
One-on-One

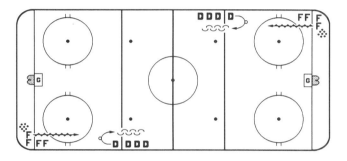

I/I 1

F starts from the corner with a puck. D should close the gap with the puck carrier by getting within stick length before too much speed is built up. D starts at the blue line and skates forward two strides inside the blue line to pick up the player coming from the corner. D now skates backward to play the one-on-one. Use both sides and start both one-on-ones at the same time.

Variation: The coach blows the whistle at mid-ice. F curls back staying on the same side, D closes the gap and the one-on-one continues.

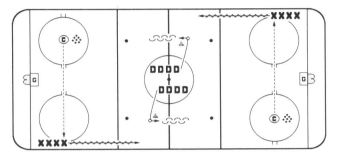

I/I 2

A coach starts the drill by passing to X on the boards. D skates laterally, pivots, and plays X one-on-one.

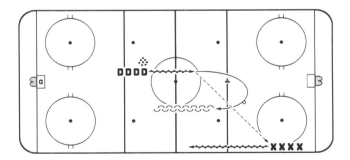

I/I 3

A player starts from the corner without a puck and receives a pass from D, who swings around the pylon at the blue line. The puck carrier skates to the far net with speed. D skates around the pylon, pivots, and plays the one-on-one.

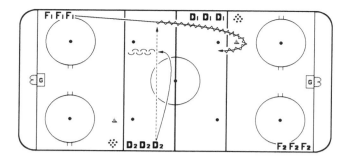

1/1 4

F1 skates up the ice receiving a pass from D2. F1 skates up around the pylon and returns to go one-on-one with D2, who has skated across to play F1 after the initial pass was made.

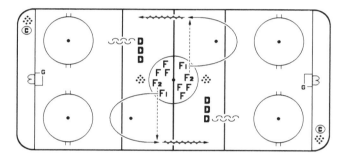

1/1 5

F1 makes a loop below the blue line, receives a pass from F2, and goes one-on-one with D. D doesn't start until F1 has the puck. A coach spots a second puck to the forward for the second one-on-one after the first shot on goal.

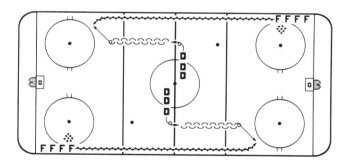

1/1 6

Position players as shown. F skates down the boards and upon reaching the far blue line drives for the goal. As F crosses the near blue line, D pivots and skates backward, playing F on the one-on-one. Use both sides of the ice at the same time.

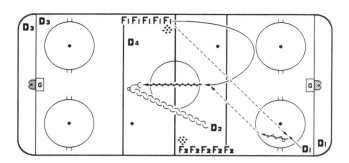

1/1 7

F1 starts with a pass to D1 in the corner. D1 steps up and passes back to the quick-breaking F1. D2 starts skating backward to play F1 when D1 steps up to make the return pass to F1.

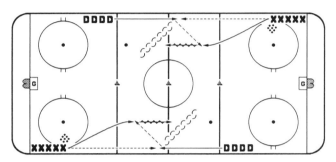

1/1 8

D starts the drill by passing to X. D then skates forward, pivots, and plays X one-on-one.

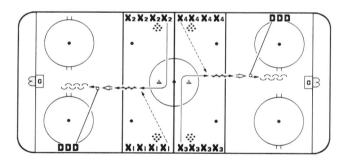

1/1 9

X2 and X3 start at the same time by skating across the ice to the middle lane, do tight turns around the pylon, and drive for the net. As they round the pylons, X2 and X3 take passes from X1 and X4 respectively. Ds are lined up by the board hash marks as shown and drive off the boards to try and stop X2 and X3 from scoring. The coach then indicates to X1 and X4 to repeat the drill.

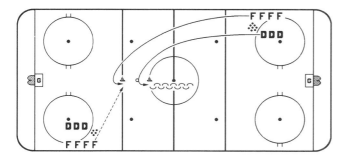

1/1 10

F1 and D1 start the drill by skating around the pylons as shown. F1 receives a pass from D2 and goes one-on-one on D1. After D2 passes the puck, D2 and F2 skate around the pylons at the center circle and the far blue line and repeat the drill, receiving a pass from the next D1.

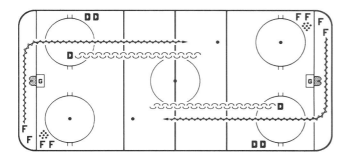

1/1 11

F skates fast behind the net and turns up the ice. As F comes out from behind the net, D starts skating backward and plays the one-on-one down the ice. Both ends can go at the same time.

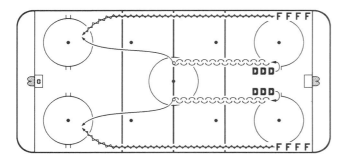

1/1 12

The players line up as shown. F drives down the boards to the far blue line then drives for the goal. As F starts, so does D, who must skate backward and cannot pivot and skate forward to take F out until he reaches the center red line.

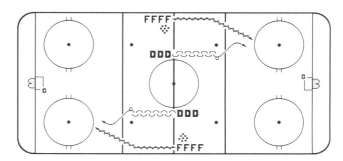

1/1 13

F and D start at the same time. D cannot turn until reaching the blue line.

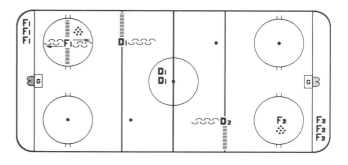

1/1 14

Both F1 and D1 move through their agility drills as shown with the forward carrying a puck. When the forward finishes the agility drill, F1 passes to D1, who passes the puck back to F1 for a one-on-one.

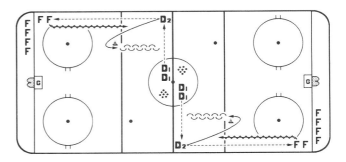

1/1 15

Position players as shown. D1 starts the drill by passing to D2. D2 passes to F, who skates forward. D1 skates backward and plays the one-on-one with F, who is coming down the boards. Both sides can go at the same time.

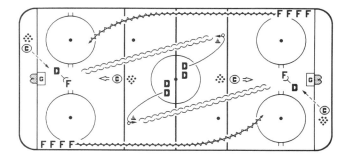

1/1 16

The D starts the drill by skating forward to the blue line, pivots, and skates backward playing F one-on-one. The coach spots a second puck for F after the first shot on goal. D defends.

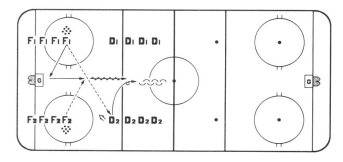

1/1 17

F1 passes to D2. F1 drives to the net for a deflection or rebound. After D2 shoots, F1 skates up-ice, receiving a pass from F2 and goes one-on-one with D2. F2 starts the next group by passing to D1.

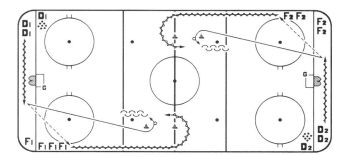

1/1 18

D1 skates behind the net with a breakout pass to F1. Both skate out to the neutral zone around the pylons and play the one-on-one. D2 and F2 start at the same time.

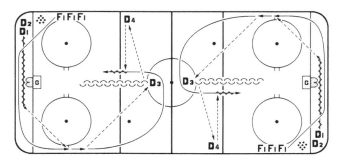

1/1 19

F1 skates hard behind the net and D1 follows. D1 passes to F1 at the hash marks. F1 quickly passes to D3. D3 passes to D4, pivots, skates backward to face F1, who receives a return pass from D4. All Ds change positions with each one-on-one.

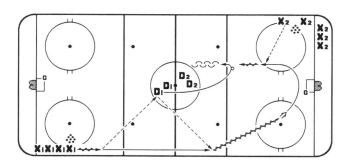

1/1 20

X1 starts the drill by passing to D1 in the circle for a give-and-go. After D1 makes the pass, D1 skates to the blue line, pivots, and plays X1, who is returning one-on-one after the shot and has picked up another puck from X2. X1 and X2 start with D1 and D2.

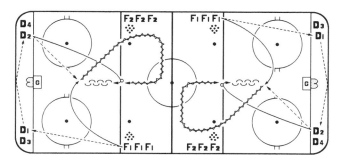

1/1 21

F1 passes to D1, who passes to D2, who in turn passes to the breaking F1. F1 skates into the neutral zone and returns one-on-one against D2. F2 starts the next one-on-one.

74

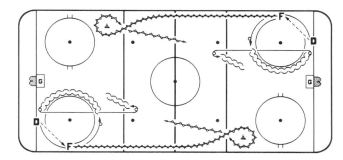

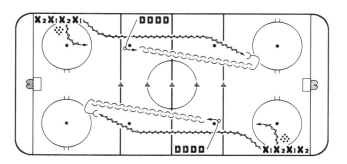

I/I 22

Position players as shown. D starts the drill by passing to F at the hash marks. F carries the puck down the boards over the far blue line, does a 360-degree tight turn around a pylon, and comes back one-on-one against D. After D has made the original pass, he skates the circle once (always facing center), then skates over the near blue line, pivots, and skates backward playing the one-on-one with F. Both sides can go at the same time.

I/I 24

D comes off the boards to play X1 one-on-one. After X1 crosses the far blue line, X2 starts another attack. The same D must also play X2 on a one-on-one. Use both sides of the ice.

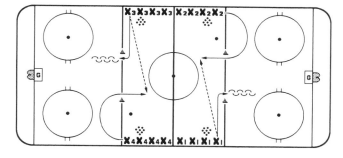

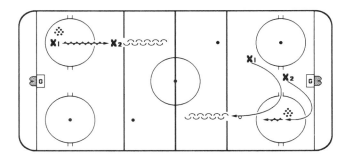

I/I 23

X1 and X3 simultaneously pass to curling X2 and X4 respectively. X1 and X3 follow their pass to the middle of the ice before they play one-on-one against X2 and X4. When the puck carrier crosses the blue line, the next group starts.

I/I 25

X1 plays X2 one-on-one. After X1 shoots, X2 picks up a puck in the circle, X2 becomes offence, and X1 becomes the defence.

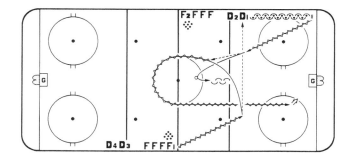

I/I 26

F1 skates over the blue line and passes wide to D1. D1 skates backward to the goal line, stops, skates forward, and passes back to F1 before F1 skates the circle. D1 skates forward to the bottom of the center-ice circle, pivots, skates backward, and plays F1 one-on-one.

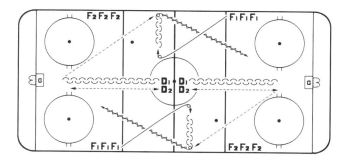

1/1 27

As Ds retreat into their respective zones, they pass a puck to each other (two pucks) before passing to F1. F1 skates to the center red line, pivots backward to the boards, and receives a pass from Ds. Ds then play Fs one-on-one in each end.

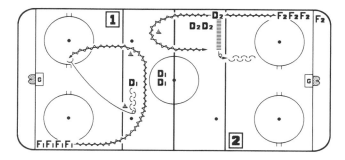

1/1 28

(1) Place the pylons as shown. F1 with a puck and D skate around the respective pylons.
(2) F skates forward around the pylon and attacks D for a one-on-one. After F crosses the blue line, D does stepovers from a stopped position to the mid-ice to play F.

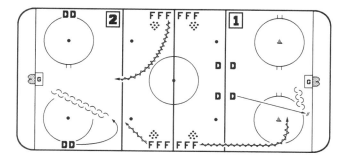

1/1 29

(1) D and F start at the same time. D rushes to the goal line, stops, and plays F breaking in from the boards.
(2) D on the hash marks skates to the top of the circle and pivots to play the incoming F one-on-one.

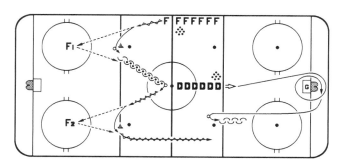

1/1 30

F and D start at the same time. D shoots on goal, skates around the net twice, and then skates up-ice to meet F one-on-one. F passes to F1 for a give-and-go, pivots, skates backward to the center-ice dot, pivots, skates forward, and passes to F2 for a second give-and-go, then skates around the pylon and goes one-on-one against D.

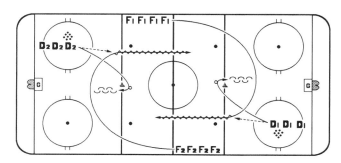

1/1 31

F1 and F2 start at the same time. D1 and D2 pass to the breaking forwards and then skate to the pylon, pivot, and play the oncoming forward one-on-one.

Variation: Use two forwards for a two-on-one.

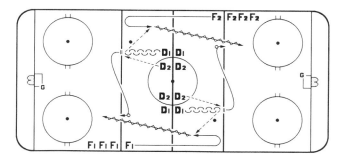

1/1 32

D1 and D2 and F1 and F2 start by skating to the blue lines. D1, on the blueline, receives a pass from D2 and quickly passes to F1 and F2, who have curled up-ice. After the pass, D1 rushes to the other side to play F one-on-one.

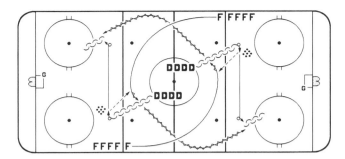

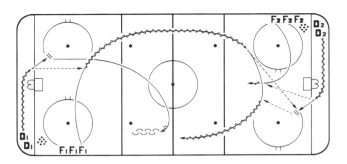

I/I 33

Place the pucks at the top of the circles as indicated. F starts at the blue line for a circular skate. D starts from the circle, skates backward to pick up a puck, and passes to the curling F. D then skates across the ice to play F coming down the opposite side.

Variation: Two forwards go two-on-one.

I/I 35

D1 skates behind the goal and passes to F1. D1 stops at the bottom of the circle and does a regroup pass with F2. F1 skates down the ice and does a regroup with D2. D2 passes to F1. D1 passes to F2. After the regroup pass, both Ds skate out to the diagonal side to play one-on-one with F1 and F2.

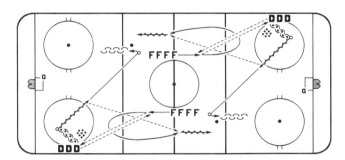

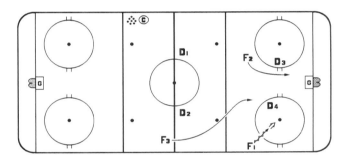

I/I 34

F skates forward, receives a pass from D but touch-passes back to D. D skates backward, pivots, then skates forward, and passes the puck to a breaking F. D now skates to the opposite side of the ice to play the oncoming F from the opposite side.

I/I 36

After the shot is taken or on a whistle, the high forward F3 in the offensive zone and D1 and D2 skate back to the zone where the coach has shot another puck. D1 or D2 retrieves the puck and sends F3 one-on-one with D3. D1 and D2 skate to the boards out of the play after the pass.

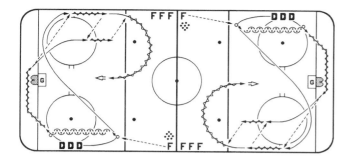 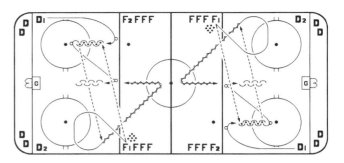

I/I 37

After F passes to D, F curls deep in the opposite corner. D receives the pass from F, pivots, and skates backward to the bottom of the circle, pivots again, and skates behind the net. D then passes to the curling F. F back-passes to D, then D passes to F again, who now goes one-on-one with D.

Variation: Do two-on-one and three-on-one.

I/I 38

D1 starts by skating to the blue line, pivots, and receives a pass from F1. F1 does an inside-out loop and receives a return pass from D1. F1 skates into the center-ice circle, does a tight turn, and goes against D1 one-on-one. D2 starts after F1 gets a shot on goal or is taken out by D1 or on the coach's signal.

12
Two- and Three-on-One

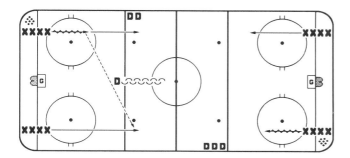

2/1 1

Two forwards break out of the zone to go two-on-one with D. Do the drill in both directions. The next group goes when the one coming down the ice has taken a shot on goal.

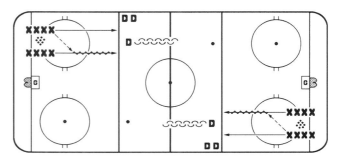

2/1 3

The two forwards go two-on-one with Ds from each side of the ice.

Variation: The forwards start at the blue line and Ds on the center red line.

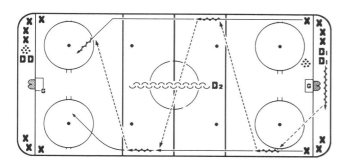

2/1 2

D1 starts the drill by passing to the winger, who goes two-on-one with D2. D1 follows up the attack to play the forwards from the other end on a two-on-one.

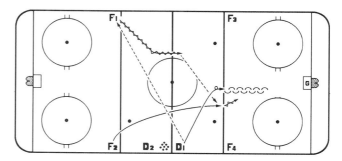

2/1 4

D1 passes to F1. After the pass, D1 skates to the middle, pivots, and plays F1 and F2 on the two-on-one. After F1 and F2 cross the blue line, D2 starts the next drill with F3 and F4.

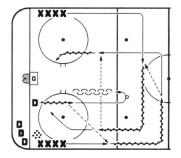

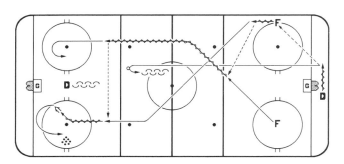

2/I 5

The D and two forwards break out. D passes to a forward, skates to the blue line, and pivots to backward skating to play the two forwards who switched sides in the neutral zone.

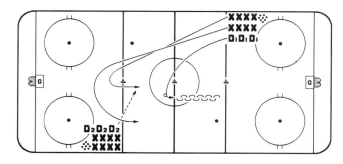

2/I 6

Two forwards skate up to the blue line, receive a pass from D2, and attack D1, who came out to center for the two-on-one.

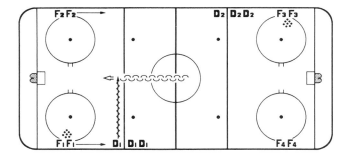

2/I 7

D1 skates across to mid-ice and shoots on goal. F1, with a puck, and F2 go two-on-one against D1. After the offensive play is finished, D2 skates across the blue line and shoots. F1 and F2 screen and deflect the shot. F3 and F4 then go two-on-one against D2.

2/I 8

D starts the play for two forwards with a breakout pass. D then skates hard for the far blue line and prepares to defend against a two-on-one on the return rush. The forwards execute a two-on-one rush. Upon completion of the two-on-one play, D defending the play picks up a puck and starts a rush the other way.

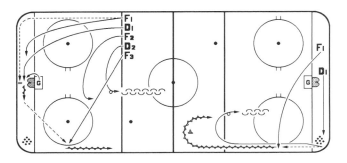

2/I 9

F1 shoots a puck around the boards and chases it. The goaltender stops the puck behind the net. D1 rushes in quickly to retrieve the puck and passes to F3, who goes with F2 for a two-on-one against D2. After the first pass, D1 retrieves a puck and passes to F1. F1 skates around the dot (or pylon) and goes one-on-one with D1.

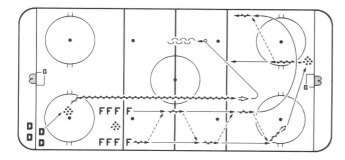

2/1 10

Two forwards start at the blue line and skate up-ice exchanging passes and finishing with a shot on goal. D follows up-ice with a puck and takes a shot on goal. The two forwards deflect and go for rebounds. D then plays the two forwards two-on-one after they picked up another puck in the corner.

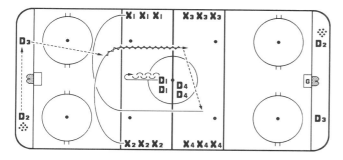

2/1 11

D2 passes to D3 for a quick breakout pass to X1 or X2. X1 and X2 go two-on-one with D1. D1 starts at center, skates to the blue line, and pivots backward to play X1 and X2. Use both ends of the ice.

Variation: Make it a three-on-one.

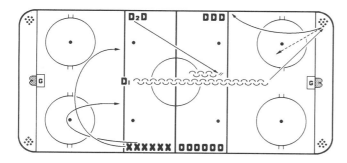

2/1 12

Two forwards, Xs, loop in as shown and go two-on-one on D1. After the play is finished, D1 then starts the next two-on-one by retrieving and passing a

puck from the corner to the next two Os who loop in from the blue line. D2 is on the blue line. D1 moves to the side boards and is replaced by another D, who follows the play to the far blue line, then plays defence for the next two-on-one. The drill is continuous.

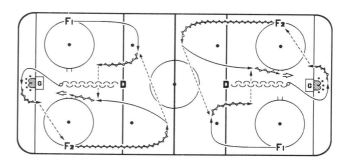

2/1 13

D starts the drill by skating behind the net, retrieving the puck and passing to F2. F2 comes outside the blue line and passes to F1 on the other side. F1 and F2 go two-on-one against D. Perform the drill in both ends of the ice.

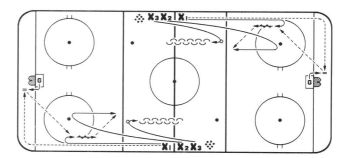

2/1 14

X1, X2, and X3 start at the same time. X1 shoots the puck into the zone. The goaltender stops the shot behind the net and passes to X1 or X2, who go back up the ice two-on-one against X3. Perform the drill on both sides of the ice.

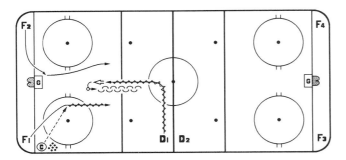

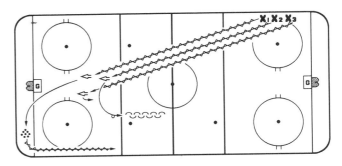

2/1 15

D1 starts the drill by skating to the center-ice face-off dot before turning up the ice and skating for the goal. On crossing the blue line, D1 takes a shot on goal. F1 and F2 start in the corners. As D1 crosses the blue line, F1 and F2 drive for the front of the net for a deflection or rebound. The coach then passes to F1 or F2, who go two-on-one against D1, who has pivoted and is skating backward down the ice.

2/1 17

X1, X2, and X3 start up-ice and each takes a shot on goal. X1 shoots and goes to the corner to retrieve a puck. X2 shoots, pivots, and prepares to play the two-on-one. X3 shoots and circles to the same side as X1 to play the two-on-one against X2. The second group starts as soon as X3 shoots.

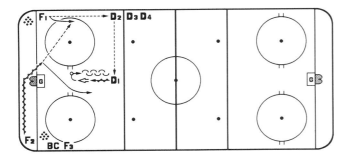

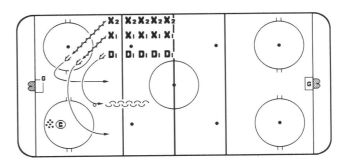

2/1 16

F1 passes to D2 and then D2 passes to D1, who moves in and takes a shot on goal. After the shot, F2 skates behind the net passing to the moving F1. F1 and F2 go two-on-one against D1. Ds rotate to the middle.

Variation: Add a backchecker for a two-on-two.

2/1 18

D1 skates over the blue line, shoots, pivots, and is ready to start playing the two-on-one. X1 shoots two seconds (count one thousand, two thousand) after D1 shoots. X2 shoots two seconds after X1. X1 or X2 will receive a pass from the coach and go two-on-one against D.

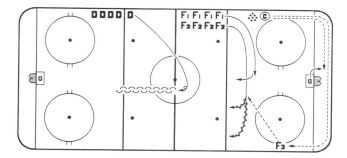

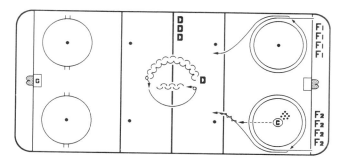

2/1 19

The coach rims the puck around the boards to F3 on the hash marks. The puck can be on the ice, off the glass, etc. F1 and F2 read the play and must time it to skate across the ice to support F3 in the breakout. D reads and skates to center to play the two- or three-on-one. While waiting for the next line to start, the coach shoots the puck behind the net for the goaltender to stop and pass back to the coach.

2/1 21

F1 and F2 start by skating the circles outside-in. D starts in the center-ice circle by skating half the circle backward, pivoting, and skating the other half of the circle forward. After skating around the circle, D pivots and skates backward, playing the two-on-one coming up-ice. The coach passes to F1 or F2.

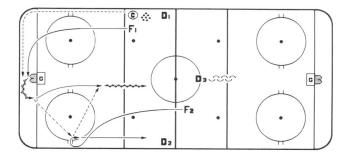

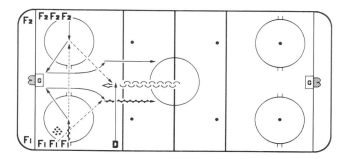

2/1 20

The coach shoots a puck into the zone and the goaltender stops the puck and sets it up behind the net. F1 or F2 retrieves the puck and breaks out two-on-one against D3.

Variation: After the pass to F3, D1 and D2 can join the rush for a two-on-one or a three-on-one.

2/1 22

F1 starts the drill with a pass to F2, who has skated to the face-off dot. F2 touch-passes to D for a shot on goal. F1 and F2 drive to the net for any rebounds. After the shot or on a whistle, F1 and F2 break out two-on-one on the D (the pass comes from line F1 on the boards).

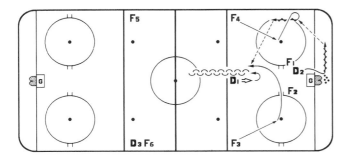

2/1 23

D1 starts the drill with a shot on goal. D2 takes F1 or F2 if there is then a rebound and retrieves a puck from behind the net and passes to F4 just below the hash marks. F4 starts up-ice and passes to F3, who has swung into the middle from the opposite boards. F3 and F4 go up-ice two-on-one on D1.

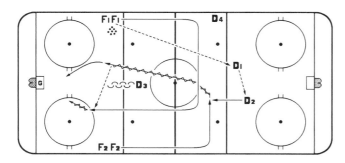

2/1 24

F1 starts the drill with a regroup pass to D1.
D1 passes to D2, D2 passes to F2, who regroups with F1 for a two-on-one on D3. D3 skates to the center-ice dot, pivots, and plays F1 and F2 two-on-one. D1 replaces D2, D2 to D3, D3 to D4, and D4 to D1.

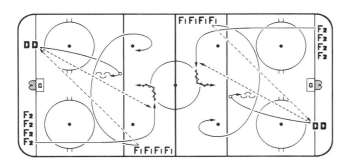

2/1 25

F1 passes to D and cuts deep but comes to regroup outside the neutral-zone face-off dot. D passes to the

curling F2, who now goes two-on-one against D, who after passing to F2 skates out to play the two-on-one.

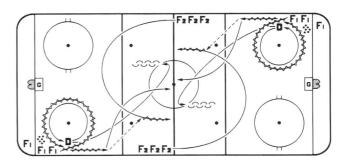

2/1 26

F1 skates around the circle protecting the puck from D, who skates around inside the circle providing passive pressure. F2 reacts to the play and uses good timing to get into position to receive a pass from F1. F1 and F2 go two-on-one with D from the opposite end. After the pass by F1, D skates to center to play the two-on-one.

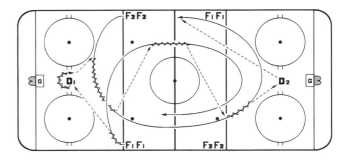

2/1 27

F1 passes to D1, who pivots. D1 passes to F2. F1 and F2 exchange passes and regroup with D2 and go two-on-one against D1.

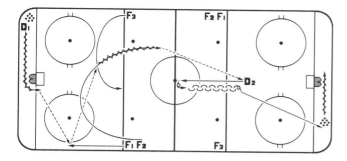

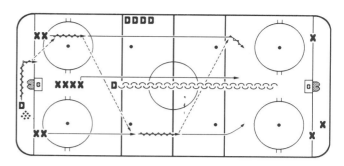

2/I 28

This is the same as the two-on-one regroup, but after D2 completes the regroup, D2 skates to center, stops, skates backward inside the blue line, pivots, and skates to the corner and starts the next two-on-one.

3/I 31

D starts the breakout of three-on-one. D continues up the ice to play the new three-on-one coming the other way. The coach can decide how the forwards will attack, i.e., carry in, delay, shoot in, etc.

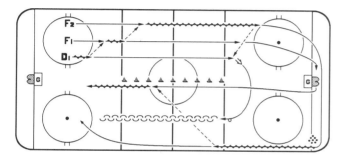

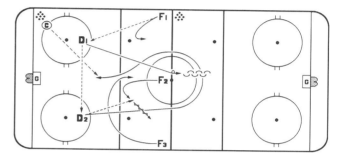

2/I 29

D1 starts the play with a pass to F1 or F2. They skate down the ice three-on-none with a pass back to D inside the blue line for a shot on goal. F1 or F2 picks up a puck in the opposite corner and goes two-on-one against D on the opposite side.

3/I 32

F1 passes to D1, who passes to D2. After passing, D1 skates hard to the center red line to play the developing three-on-one. Forwards F1, F2, and F3 loop and do the regroup and attack three-on-one. After passing to F2 or F3, D2 skates hard around the center-ice circle and goes in for a shot at the same end after receiving a pass from the corner.

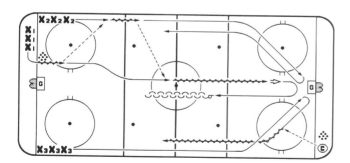

2/I 30

The players skate down the ice three-on-zero but return two-on-one with the high forward becoming a defensive player.

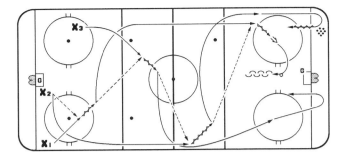

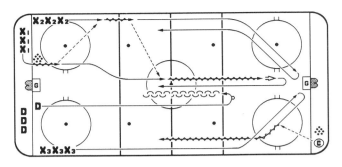

3/I 33

XI cuts across to the middle, X2 passes to XI, and
X2 fills the XI lane. XI passes to X3, cutting into the
middle. XI fills the X3 lane, etc. The players fill the
lane that was left vacant and the player without the
puck always cuts behind the player with the puck.
Finish with a shot on goal. After the shot on goal,
one of the attackers becomes a defenceman for a
two-on-one back into the other end.

3/I 34

The players attack four-on-zero but come back three-
on-one. D skates to the opposite blue line with or
just behind the rush, pivots, and skates backward,
playing the three-on-one.

13

Two- and Three-on-Two

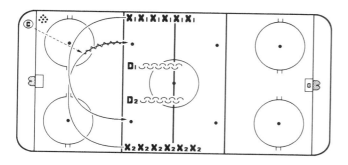

2/2 1

D1 and D2 start on the blue line on their knees. On the whistle, X1 and X2 swing across the ice, receiving a pass from the coach in the corner. D1 cannot get up until a forward receives the pass. X1 and X2 go two-on-two against the D.

Variation: Add a backchecker and release another player from line X1 or X2. After X1 and X2 cross the blue line, the extra players are released for a three-on-three.

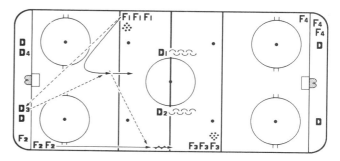

2/2 2

Position players as shown. F1 passes to D3. F1 curls to receive a pass back from D3. F1 and F2 then attack D1 and D2 for a two-on-two. D3 and D4 move up to the opposite blue line to play F3 and F4 on the return two-on-two.

Variation: Play F1 to D4 to D3 to F1.

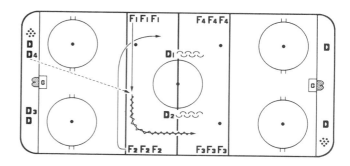

2/2 3

F1 and F2 do a wide swing and receive a pass from D4 for a two-on-two attack against D1 and D2. D3 and D4 skate to the blue line for the next attack from F3 and F4.

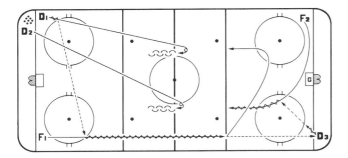

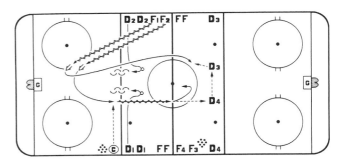

2/2 4

D1, D2, and F1 start the drill at the same time. D1 passes rink-wide to F1, who carries up the ice to the far blue line. F1 then passes to D3, who in turn passes to a curling F2. After passing to D3, F1 curls up-ice and goes with F2 two-on-two against D1 and D2. After making the initial pass, D1 and D2 skate up-ice past the center red line, pivot, and play the two-on-two against F1 and F2.

2/2 7

F1 and F2 shoot on goal with F2 shooting first and then they curl up-ice. F2 receives a pass from the coach. F2 feeds a pass to D4, who passes to D3, who then passes to the curling F1 or F2. F1 and F2 then attack D1 and D2, who have skated to the center-ice circle, pivoted, and are set to play the two-on-two. F3 and F4 then start.

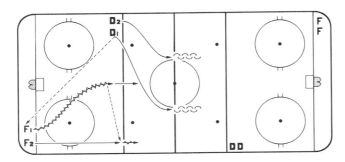

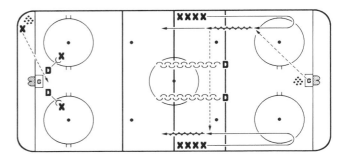

2/2 5

D1 starts the play by passing to F1 in the corner. F1 and F2 come out of the zone and go two-on-two with D1 and D2. D1 and D2 close the gap.

2/2 8

Two X players skate into the zone to the hash marks, curl up-ice, receive a pass from the goaltender and attack two-on-two. After a goal or a whistle, the coach passes a puck to one of the offensive players.

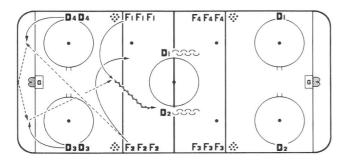

2/2 6

F2 starts the drill with a pass to D4, D4 passes behind the net to D3, who passes to a curling F1 and F2. F1 and F2 go two-on-two against D1 and D2. D3 and D4 move up to play F3 and F4 on the next rush.

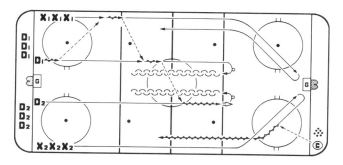

2/2 9

Two Ds skate to the far blue line and then pivot and skate backward. X1 and X2 start at the same time, skate to the far goal, do tight turns and go two-on-two.

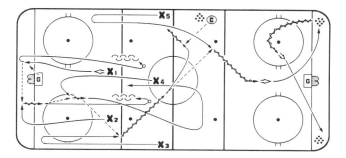

3/2 10

X1 starts the drill with a shot on goal. X1 and X2 retrieve a puck and X2 passes to a curling center X4, X4 passes to X3, who passes to the fast-breaking X5. X5 goes in for a shot then retrieves a puck in each corner for a second, then third shot. X3 and X4 receive a pass in the neutral zone from the coach and attack two-on-two against X1 and X2.

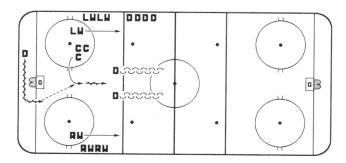

3/2 11

D behind the goal starts the three-on-two with a pass to the center or one of the wingers. The next group of players gets in position when the three-on-two moves over the center red line. Rotate defensive and offensive defence.

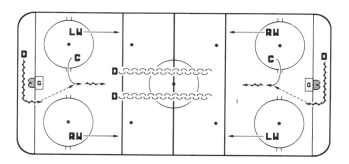

3/2 12

Two forward lines are in the end where the drill starts and one forward line is at the other end. After the first three-on-two, a new line breaks out and the first line stays in the end where it finished the drill.

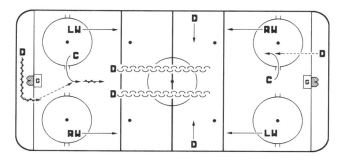

3/2 13

This is the same as the previous drill but the same line attacks continuously three-on-two in both ends until the coach signals for the next line.

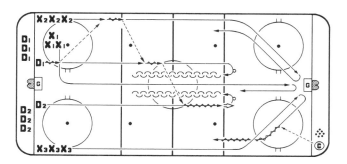

3/2 14

X1, X2, and X3 skate to the far goal and D1 and D2 skate up to the blue line to play the three-on-two. D1 starts the drill with a pass to the board-side player for a return pass to D1. D1 passes to D2. At the blue line, the forwards drive to the net before the shot from D1 or D2 and then come back with a pass from the coach for a three-on-two.

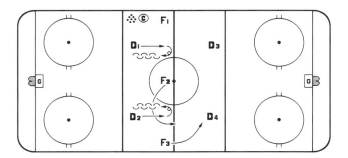 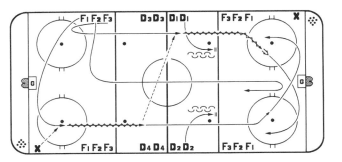

3/2 15

Position the players as shown. On the whistle, D1 and D2 skate to the center red line, pivot, and skate backward to the blue line. The coach shoots a puck into the corner. D1 or D2 retrieve it with light pressure from one of the forwards. D1 and D2 set up the breakout for a three-on-two on D3 and D4.

3/2 16

The three forwards start the drill at the same time and go down three-on-zero at the far end. F2 and F3 must watch their speed coming out of the zone. As they pass D1 and D2, the two Ds skate to the blue line, stop, and start backward skating to play the three-on-two. The forwards, after shooting on goal, change positions with the two wingers criss-crossing and the center doing a tight turn. The coach passes to F1 and the line starts the three-on-two.

14
Warmup

SKATING AND PASSING WARMUPS
WU 1

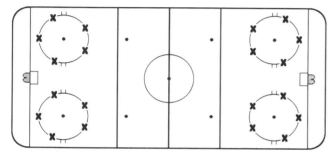

The players do touch-passing around the circle with one player in the middle.

Variation: The players are down on their knees passing the puck around.

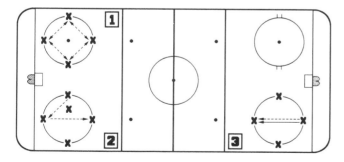

WU 2

Players practice one-touch passing in the circles.
(1) Touch-pass to each other.
(2) Follow your pass.
(3) Pass through the middle with a defender in the middle.

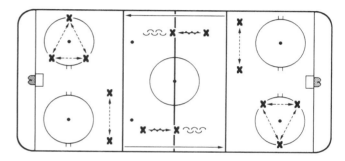

WU 3

Two players pass the puck. One skates forward, the other backward. Three players pass in a triangle. Players skate around the rink all doing the same drill at one time.

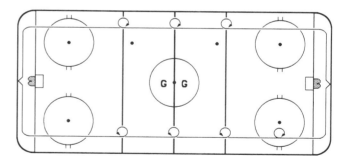

WU 4

The players skate the outside perimeter doing 360-degree inside-out or outside-in turns at the blue lines and center red line. As the players skate behind the net, they throw themselves at the boards as if shoulder-checking another player and continue skating after the check.

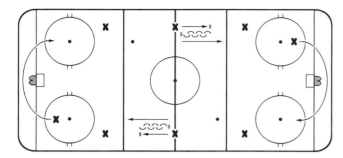

WU 5

All players skate around the rink and on the whistle take three quick forward strides, stop, three steps backward, stop, three quick strides forward, and then skate easy until the next whistle. This drill will help develop quick feet.

Variation: Do with pucks or make it a four-four-four drill.

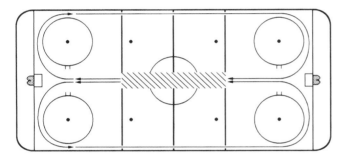

WU 6

Stretch the major muscle groups of the lower body while skating down the middle of the ice. The upper body muscles are stretched while skating down the outside of the ice. When players are turning at the bottom and top of the circles, push hard off the edges to pick up speed. Players switch sides as they come out of the middle lane.

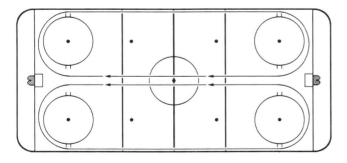

WU 7

Using the same formation, incorporate speed intervals to warm up the body, emphasizing proper skating technique in pushes, full leg extension, and

proper turns. Players switch sides each time they come out of the middle lane of the butterfly.

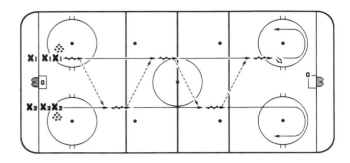

WU 8

Both players skate down the ice, passing as many times as possible, with a shot at the inside hash marks at the far end. Players return along the perimeter of the ice doing light stretches and switch lines on their return.

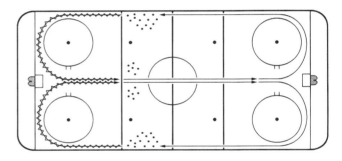

WU 9

Players pick up the puck at the blue line while skating the outside as shown and when skating up the middle pass to the side boards before crossing the blue line. Add variations such as skating backward, pivots, etc.

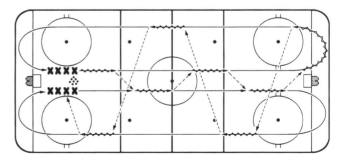

WU 10

The players pass the puck to each other in the middle and then do wide passing returning on the outside. Include your goaltenders in this drill. Switch lines on return in order that forehand and backhand passes are executed. Increase speed between the blue lines.

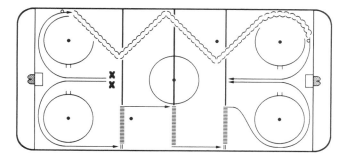

WU 11

Add variations to the down-the-middle warmup such as turns, pivots, backwards skating, cross-steps, etc.

Variation: Repeat after warmup using pucks.

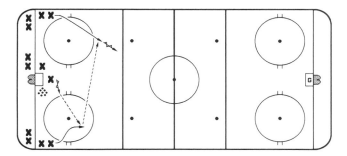

WU 12

Three players must make three passes in each zone, namely before the blue line, blue line to the center red line, the center red line to the far blue line, and the far blue line to the end of the ice. Repeat coming the other way.

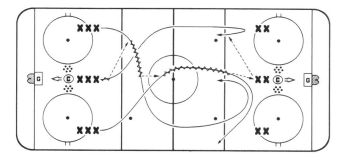

WU 13

Three players pass, interchanging positions and regroup with a pass to the player in the middle line at the opposite end of the ice. The three players at the opposite end of the ice then start a three-man weave. Coaches warm up the goaltenders at each end.

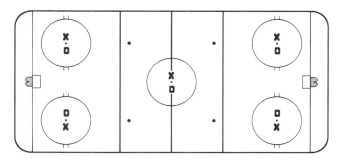

WU 14

The players are paired together and the player with the puck tries to use good puck protection to keep the puck away from the attacker. Do the drills for 10 seconds. Try to place players in circles so they are forced to work in a confined area.

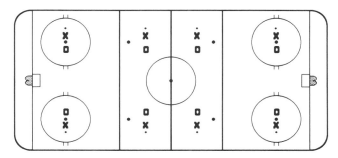

WU 15

The players line up in pairs with a defensive player and an offensive player. The defensive player has no stick and the puck is placed behind the defensive player. On the whistle, the offensive players try to retrieve the puck behind the defensive player. Do the drill for 10 seconds then rest.

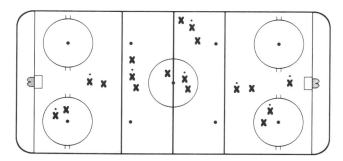

WU 16

The players skate around the ice with eight of them having a puck. If another player wants a puck, it must be taken from one of the players with a puck. Players go full speed on the whistle.

SKATING, PASSING, AND SHOOTING WARMUPS

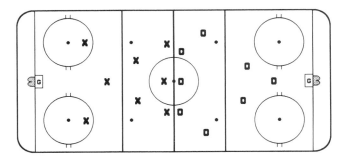

WU 17

Divide your team into two groups (usually about eight per side). The warmup is a scrimmage with the first team to score three goals being the winner. No body contact or slap shots are allowed.

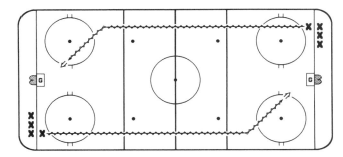

WU 18

Divide the players into groups. The players skate the full length of the ice and shoot on the goaltender. The shot can be designated by pylons on the ice. Switch sides halfway through the drill.

Variation: Pass to another player on the way down the ice and take a return pass for a give-and-go.

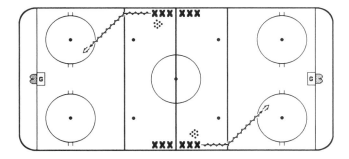

WU 19

The players skate in a continuous line from the right or left side and shoot wrist shots in rapid succession.

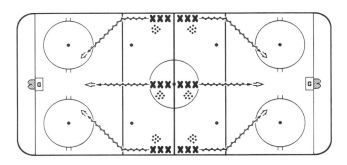

WU 20

A player from each line shoots wrist shots from the top of the circles. Switch lines as the players return.

Variation: The first line shoots from the top of the circle, the middle line shoots from the slot, and the third line skates in and dekes. The players switch lines when they return.

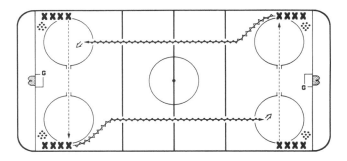

WU 21

The player in one corner passes across to the player in the opposite corner, who skates wide down the boards and shoots.

Variation: The player in the opposite corner skates to the middle, receives a pass, skates down the opposite side of the ice, and shoots.

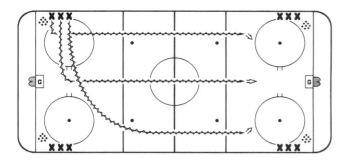

WU 22

Three players start at the same time with one player shooting from each lane when they reach the far blue line.

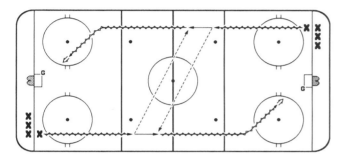

WU 23

The players start at the same time from opposite corners, each carrying pucks. Between the blue lines, each player passes the puck to the other player and then continues on and shoots after receiving the pass. The players move to the opposite corners after shooting.

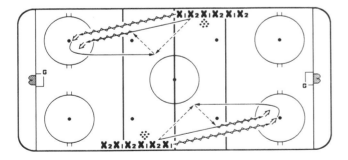

WU 24

X1 skates and shoots, turns back, and receives a pass from X2. X1 touch-passes back to X2, who skates in and shoots.

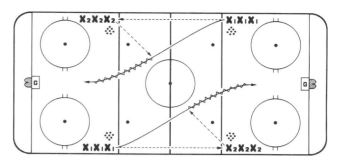

WU 25

X1 does a give-and-go with X2, and X2 touch-passes back to X1. X1 takes a shot on goal. X2 now does the same pattern with X1. Use both sides of the ice.

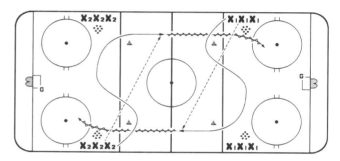

WU 26

Both X players skate the "S" pattern and receive a pass from their respective groups. After receiving a puck, the player takes a shot on goal. When X1 crosses the blue line, X2 does the same pattern.

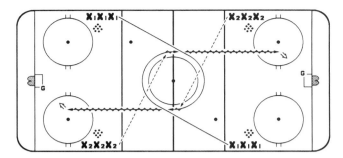

WU 27

X1 players go at the same time and receive passes from X2 players while skating around the circle. X1 players then go in for a shot on goal. X2 starts when X1 crosses the blue line.

Variation: Players skate counter-clockwise.

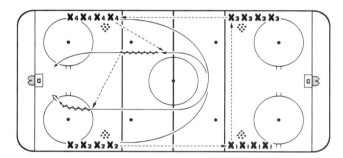

WU 28

Set up players on each blue line as shown. X2 passes to X1. X2 and X4 start at the same time to skate around the circle. The passing sequence is X2 to X1, X1 to X3, X3 to X4, and X4 does a touch-pass to X2. After X2 and X4 have made the neutral zone curl for the regroup, they finish with a two-on-zero. X1 starts the next sequence.

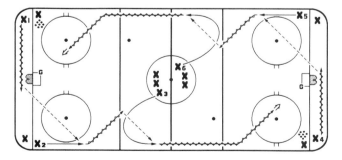

WU 29

Position players on ice as indicated. X1 and X4 start at the same time. X1 passes to X2, who cuts towards

the middle. X3 leaves the circle curling inside-out to the boards, timing it to receive a pass from X2. X1 goes to X2, X2 goes to X3, and X3 goes in for a shot on goal. X3 will then go to X4's line.

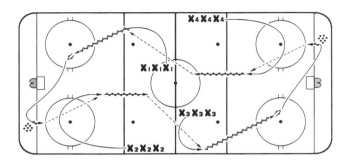

WU 30

X1 shoots, goes to the corner, and passes to the looping X2. X2 passes to the curling X3, who shoots, picks up a puck, and passes to X4, etc.

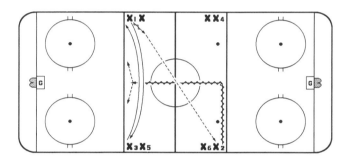

WU 31

X1, after passing diagonally to X2, swings wide with X3. X2 brings the puck through center ice and attacks three-on-zero with X1 and X3. After X2 crosses the blue line, X4 starts the drill in the opposite direction.

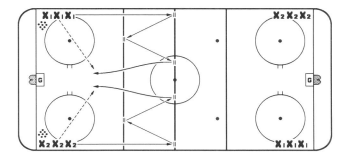

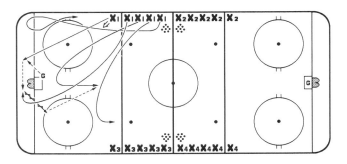

WU 32

The players skate to the center red line, stop, skate back to the blue line, stop, skate to the center red line again, stop, and drive down the middle to receive a pass from the corner and finish with a shot on goal.

WU 33

The first player shoots the puck to the goaltender, who places it behind the net. The first player skates in to retrieve the puck as the four other players go to a breakout position. The breakout is executed and the players go five-on-zero down the ice.

15

Neutral Zone: Regroups

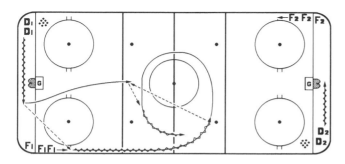

NZ 1

D1 starts the drill with a pass to F1. F1 skates into the neutral zone and passes back to D1. F1 skates the center-ice circle and receives a pass back from D1 to go one-on-zero.

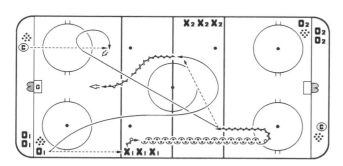

NZ 2

O1 passes to X1, who skates backward with the puck to the face-off circle in the far end. X1 then pivots and skates out over the blue line and passes to O1. X1 then skates across the ice and into the zone and curls. A coach passes the puck to X1, who then takes a shot on goal. After making the initial

pass, O1 skates to the center red line, goes around the face-off circle, and heads into the zone taking a pass from X1. O1 takes a shot on goal.

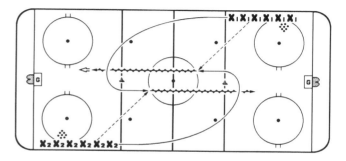

NZ 3

The players skate down the boards, swing inside the blue line around the pylon, and receive a pass from the boards to go down the ice for a shot on goal.

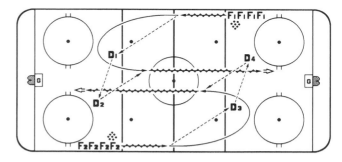

NZ 4

This is similar to the previous drill but adds defence. F1 passes to D1, who in turn passes to D2. D2 passes back to F1 after the turn below D1. F1 takes a shot on goal.

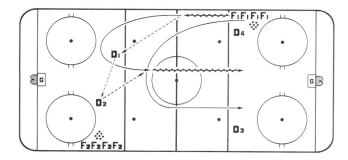

NZ 5

This is similar to the previous drill but two forwards now go instead of one. The first forward goes deep around D1 and the second forward goes wide through the middle.

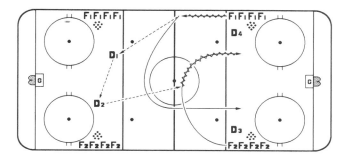

NZ 6

F1 and F2 pass to D1 and D2 and swing through the neutral zone to receive a pass back from D to complete the regroup.

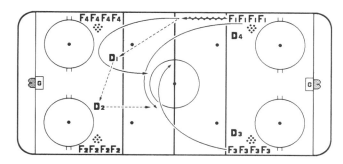

NZ 7

In this drill, three forwards swing through the neutral zone and then attack the goal.

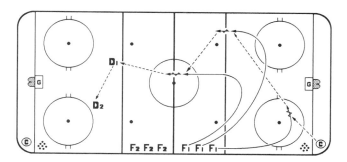

NZ 8

Three forwards skate into the zone, receive a pass from the coach, do a regroup with D1 and D2, and attack the zone three-on-zero.

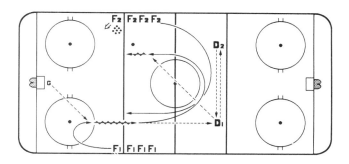

NZ 9

F2 starts the drill with a shot on the goaltender, who passes to a curling F1. F1 passes to D1, D1 to D2, and D2 back to D1. D1 passes to F1, who is curling with F2. F1 and F2 go two-on-zero. F1 starts the next group with a shot on the goaltender.

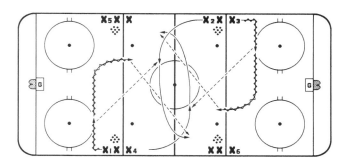

NZ 10

X1 and X2 skate laterally across the ice. X1 can pass to X2 early or after X2 has curled up-ice. X1 and X2 go two-on-zero on the goaltender. X3 and X4 go next.

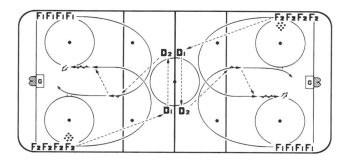

NZ 11

F1 starts the drill with a pass to D1, who passes to D2. D2 passes to F1 or F2, who loop in to the offensive zone, receive a pass, and go two-on-zero. Use both ends of the ice at the same time.

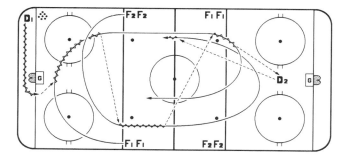

NZ 12

D1 skates behind the net and passes to F2. F1 and F2 cross, regroup with D2, and go two-on-one against D1.

Variation: Add two defence and an extra forward.

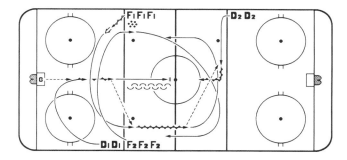

NZ 13

F1 shoots the puck at the goaltender. D1 loops into the zone and takes a pass from the goaltender and passes to F1 or F2, who does a double swing. F1 skates to the center red line and passes to D2, who is now in position. D2 passes to F1 or F2 on the regroup. After the pass to F1, D1 moves up to center ice to play F1 and F2 on the regroup.

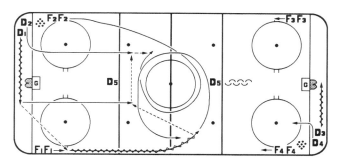

NZ 14

Position players as shown. D1 starts the drill by carrying the puck behind the goal. As D1 comes out the far side of the goal, a pass is made to F1 at the hash marks. F1 skates up-ice and after crossing the center red line drops a pass to D1, who has followed the play up to the blue line. D1 passes to D2, who then passes to F2 on the regroup. F2 starts the drill at the same time as F1, and as both cross the center red line, they skate the center-ice circle. As they finish skating the circle, F1 and F2 head up the ice again with F2 taking the pass from D2. F1 and F2 attack the zone two-on-one against D5.

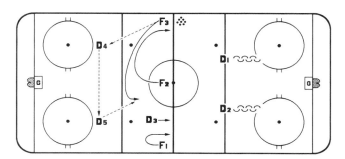

NZ 15

Position players as shown. F3 starts the drill by passing to D4, who passes to D5. F3 loops into the center lane. X2 reads that the center loop will be filled and loops to the open lane that F3 left. F1 delays, curls, and heads up the ice. D5 passes to F3 and all three forwards attack D1 and D2 in the other end of the ice. Rotate the defence around so they have offensive and defensive responsibilities.

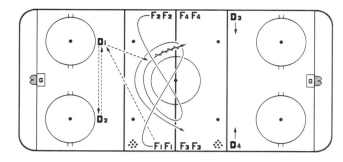

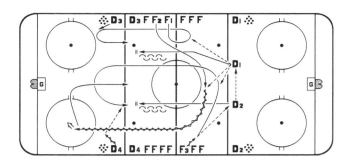

NZ 16

F1 starts with a diagonal pass to D1. D1 and D2 pass twice, ending up with D1 passing to F2, who has looped into the zone with F1. F1 and F2 go for a two-on-zero against the goaltender at the far end. F3 or F4 starts next with D3 and D4.

NZ 19

D1 and D2 start on the blue line. F3 starts the drill with a pass to D2 and then D2 to D1. D1 passes to F3, F2, or F1. (In this case, F2 receives the pass.) All three forwards go three-on-zero. After the shot, the three forwards regroup, receive a pass from D4, and go three-on-two with D1 and D2, who have moved up to the blue line to play the three-on-two.

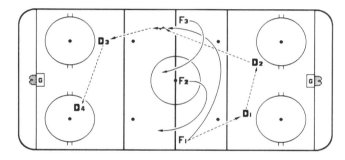

NZ 17

F1, F2, and F3 do a double regroup with D1 and D2 and then regroup with D3 and D4 and then attack three-on-zero.

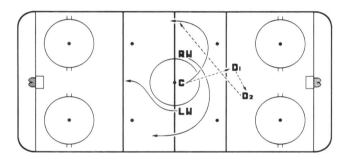

NZ 20

Regroup from a faceoff. The C draws the puck back to D1. D1 passes to D2 and D2 passes back to the center who has curled towards the boards after winning the draw.

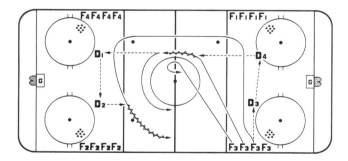

NZ 18

Three forwards (F3 line) start by passing to D3, who passes to D4. D4 passes the puck back to one F3 and they then do another regroup with D1 and D2 before attacking three-on-one.

16
Breakouts

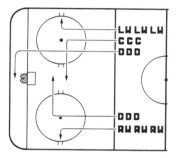

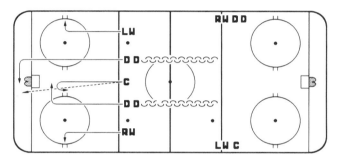

BO 1

The players line up in lines and defence pairs against the boards outside the blue line. The centers line up on the boards with either wing. The lines and defence pairs go in order and the puck is shot into the defensive zone by the coach. The coach indicates the method of bringing the puck out of the end.

BO 3

Line up the players, by position as shown at the blue line. The puck is shot in by the center and the first player in each line moves in to bring the puck out. The coach designates the method of bringing the puck out of the end. The breakout progresses the length of the ice as a five-on-two. When the offensive play is completed, another breakout starts from the opposite end using another offensive line and defence pair starting at the far blue line. The defence pair who started the play follows it down the ice and then acts defensively for the next five-on-two.

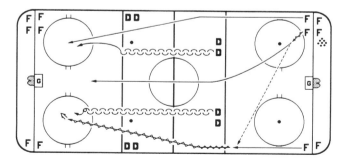

BO 2

The drill starts with a three-on-two from one end. After the shot, on the whistle, three new forwards break out in the opposite direction on a new set of defence.

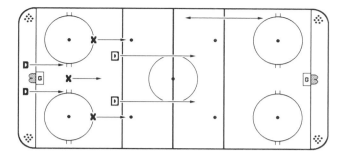

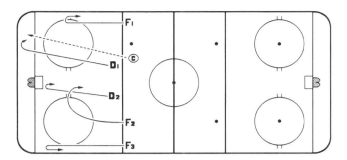

BO 4

Place four defence and one forward line on the ice as shown. One of the Ds passes the puck to a forward and they come out quickly five-on-two. They attack the opposing D for one scoring opportunity, then pick up a loose puck in the corner and start the drill the other way. The players continue to go five-on-two for a maximum of two minutes. Change lines.

BO 6

The coach shoots a puck in for a five-on-zero breakout. As the players break out, they pass the puck to the coach. The coach repeats the shoot-in three times before the players go five-on-zero down the ice and attack the far goal.

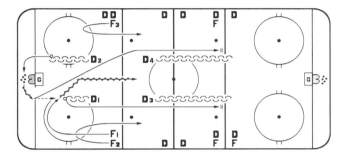

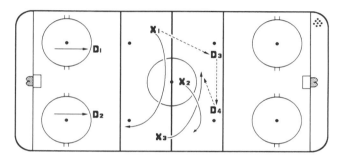

BO 5

Position the four Ds and forwards as shown. On the whistle, D1 and D2 skate backward with D2 picking up a puck and feeding a curling F1 through the middle for a three-on-two or five-on-two against D3 and D4. After the shot or on a whistle, D3 and D4 set up a breakout for the forwards for a three-on-two or a five-on-two against D1 and D3. The drill continues until the coach signals a line change.

BO 7

D1, D2, X1, X2, and X3 break out, regroup with D3 and D4 and then with D1 and D2 for a five-on-zero (D3 and D4 step out for the five-on-zero). D1 and D2 skate through to the opposite corners and start the next breakout with X1, X2, and X3. D3 and D4 come back in for the two regroups finishing with a five-on-zero and a second point shot after a pass from the coach.

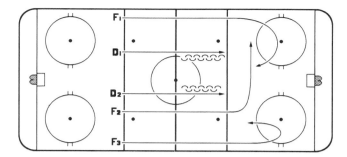

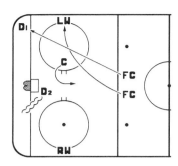

BO 8

The players break out five-on-zero and on the whistle or a score, return for a three-on-two attack against the D who followed up ice on the breakout.

BO 11

Break out five against two forecheckers.
The coach shoots the puck in and the defence must read the pressure and pick options available.

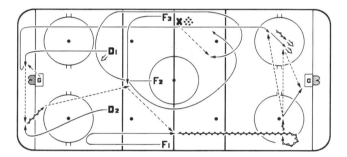

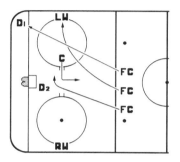

BO 9

D1 shoots on goal then retrieves the puck and passes to D2, in the opposite corner. F1, F2, and F3 skate into the zone. F2 and F3 switch lanes. D2 passes to F3 and then F3 to F1. F1 goes wide and deep, delays, and passes to a late-coming D1. F2 and F3 regroup at the blue line, receive a puck from the coach, and go two-on-one against D2.

BO 12

Break out five against three forecheckers.
The coach shoots the puck in and the defence must read the type of forechecking and react accordingly with the proper breakout.

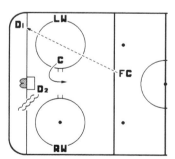

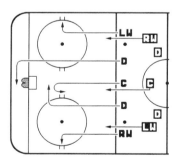

BO 10

Break out five against one forechecker.
The coach shoots the puck in and the defence must always read the forechecking before moving the puck.

BO 13

Break out five-against-five.
The breakout group starts on the blue line and the forechecking group starts halfway between the blue line and the center line. The coach shoots the puck in to start the drill. The drill can end when the one group breaks out or the forechecking teams score or the puck is frozen for a faceoff.

Variation: After the puck is shot in, the play continues for a designated time (20 or 30 seconds).

17
Specialty Teams: Power Play, Penalty Killing

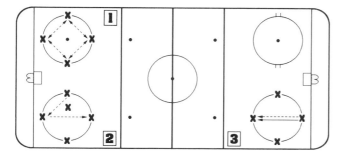

PP 1

The players practice one-touch passing in the circles.
(1) Touch-pass to each other.
(2) Follow your pass.
(3) Pass through the middle with a defender in the middle.

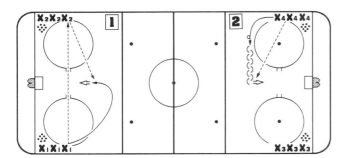

PP 2

Forward Shooting Lead Up Drills.
(1) The players pass across the ice, move to the slot for a return pass from the boards, and take a one-time shot on goal.
(2) The players come off the boards, pivot, and shoot a one-timer off the pass.

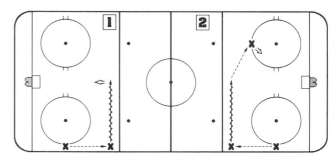

PP 3

(1) The player (defenceman) receives a pass from the hash marks, moves across the blue line to mid-ice, and shoots.
(2) The player (defenceman) moves to the middle lane and makes a quick pass to the player on the top of the circle for a shot on goal.

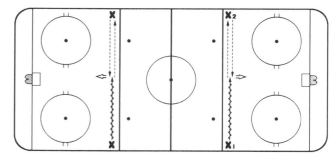

PP 4

The defenceman moves laterally. X1 starts on the boards, and X2 stands in the middle. As X1 moves towards the middle, X2 skates backward to the opposite boards. X1 passes to X2, who passes back to the middle for a shot on goal.

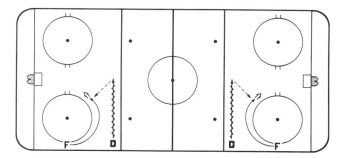

PP 5

D carries the puck to the mid-lane and passes to F, coming off the boards, for a shot on goal.

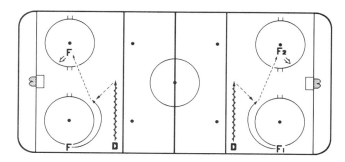

PP 6

D skates to the middle but passes back to F1 coming off the boards. F1 quickly passes to F2 for a shot on goal. The left shot D passes to left shot F1, the right shot D passes to the right shot F. Change so that the left shot D passes to the right shot F.

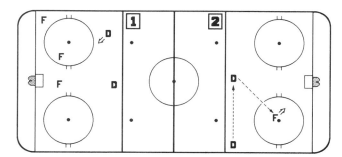

PP 7

(1) D shoots and the three forwards jam the net. Use wrist shots for quick shots on the net.
(2) D passes to D who passes to F (left shot) on the face-off dot. F then shoots a one-timer (shoots without stopping the puck).

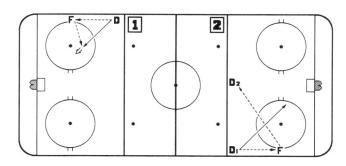

PP 8

(1) D does a give-and-go with F and shoots.
(2) Give-and-go pass to the off-side D. After D1 passes to F1, D1 goes to the net. F passes to D2 who then can shoot or pass.

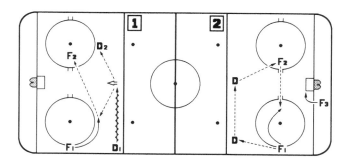

PP 9

(1) After D moves the puck to the middle, D1 has the option to pass back to F1, pass to D2, pass to F2, or shoot on goal.
(2) Pass back to the back side. F1 passes to D, who passes to the other D, who passes to F2. F2 passes to F1 (left shot) who has moved in the circle. F3 tries to jam in the rebound.

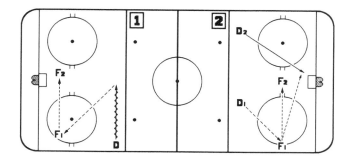

PP 10

(1) D moves to the middle and passes to F1 (right shot), who quickly passes to F2 (left shot).
(2) Slot power play. D1 passes to F1. F1 can pass to F2 in the slot or to D2 driving to the net.

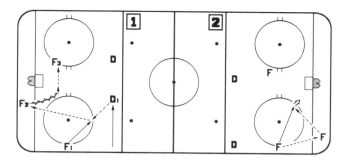

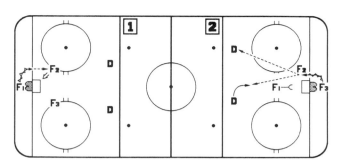

PP 11

(1) F1 passes to F2 beside the goal. F2 moves out in front of the net and passes to F3 starting on the circle or that area between the dot and the circle. F2 can also shoot on net instead of passing.

(2) Two forwards do a give-and-go from the corner.

PP 14

(1) F1 moves out from behind the net and passes to F2. F2 can either shoot or pass to F3 for the shot.

(2) F3 starts from behind the net and moves to one side and passes to F2, or F3 can also move out to pass to either D. F1 and F2 can screen and pick.

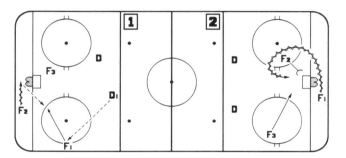

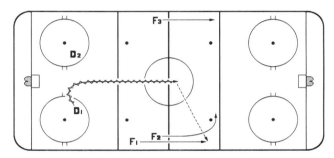

PP 12

(1) D1 passes to F1, who passes to F2. F2 skates towards the back of the goal and back-passes to F1 driving to the goal.

(2) F2 runs a pick for F1, who is coming out from behind the net for a shot on goal.

PP 15

Power-play breakout, quick turn up.

Practice different power-play breakouts depending on the forechecking pressure. D carries to center and passes to F1, while F2 cuts across at the blue line. Practice the breakouts five-on-zero first, then go five-on-two.

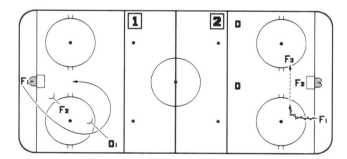

PP 13

(1) F2 and D1 run picks (block outs) so F1 can swing around as shown for a shot on goal.

(2) With F2 in front of the net, F1 makes a quick pass to F3 (right shot) for a shot on goal.

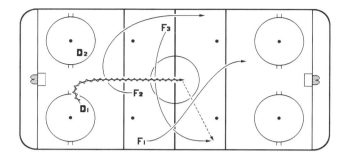

PP 16
Power-play breakout, quick turn up.
D1 turns up-ice after retrieving the puck and has a number of options available. D1 can pass to F3 as shown or carry the puck up to the blue line and make a play. Practice five-on-zero, then five-on-two.

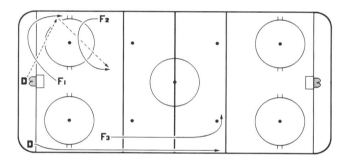

PP 17
Power-play breakout, double swing.
D passes to F1, who has curled low in the corner. F1 moves the puck to F2, who has come off the boards. Practice five-on-zero, then five-on-two.

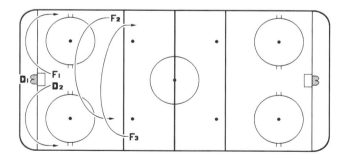

PP 18
Power-play breakout, double swing, forwards cross.
D is behind the goal and has the option to pass to either the swinging F or D or pass to either of the forwards, F1 or F2 curling high, or D1 can carry the puck out. Practice five-on-zero, then five-on-two.

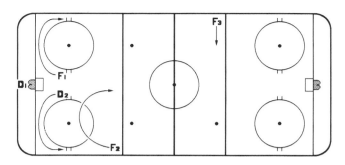

PP 19
Power-play breakout, double swing with a forward high.
D1 stands behind the net with the puck as D2 and F1 do a double swing around the bottom of the circles. F2 is on the boards at the near blue line with F3 on the boards at the far blue line, thus stretching out the opposition defence. Perform the drill five-on-zero, then five against two Ds.

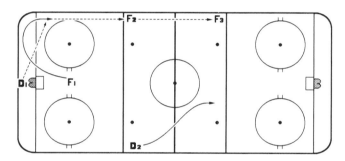

PP 20
Power-play breakout, single swing, forward to forward.
D1 stands behind the net with the puck. F1 swings into the corner, receives a pass from D1, and passes to F2 at the blue line, who in turn passes to F3 at the far blue line. Perform the drill five-on-zero, then five-against-two.

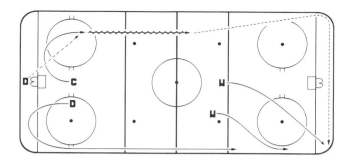

PP 21
Power-play breakout, double swing with a rim-the-puck shoot-in.

After receiving the puck, F1 skates across the center red line and sends a hard rim shot in around the boards. Keep the puck high and hard to reduce the chance of the goaltender playing the puck. F2 and F3 skate hard to retrieve the puck. Perform the drill five-on-zero, then five-against-two.

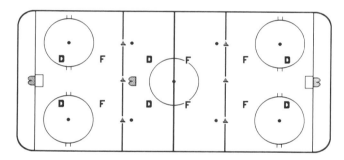

PP PK 22
Penalty killing.

Set up the box formation in all three zones and have the players move to react to the puck position on the coach's signals.

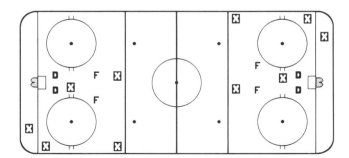

PP PK 23
Penalty killing.

Position the penalty killers without sticks against the power-play group.

Variation: Do five-on-three, five-on-four, etc., with and without sticks for the penalty killers.

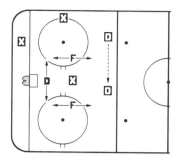

PP PK 24
Three-on-five using the triangle, rotating triangle, or the sliding triangle.

In the sliding triangle (as shown), the D covers the front of the net from one side to the other depending on puck position and the two other defenders slide back and forth.

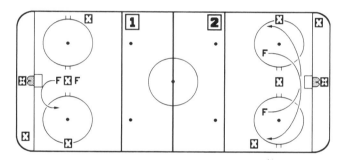

PP PK 25
Penalty killing forechecking.

Practice power-play breakouts against two types of forechecking.

(1) Stack formation: Forecheckers line up behind each other.

(2) Swing formation: The first forechecker swings one way, the other forechecker swings the other way.

18
Defensive Zone

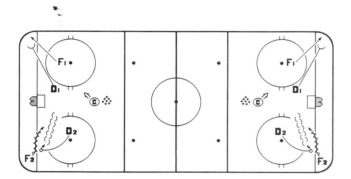

DZ 1

D1 and F1 are on one knee. The coach shoots the puck into the corner. Give D1 the advantage, then give F1 the advantage of getting to the puck first. In another drill in the other corner F2 starts with puck, D2 moves towards F2 and then skates backward and prevents F2 from going to the net.

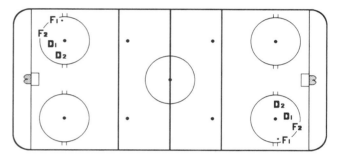

DZ 3

Defensive-zone coverage lead up drill.
The players are on one knee. The first defenceman D1 goes for the puck carrier F1 while the second defenceman D2 holds and goes for the second forward F2 when the puck is passed.

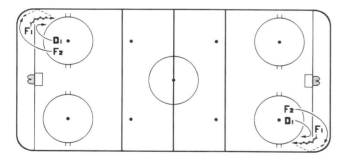

DZ 2

Defensive-zone coverage lead up drill.
F1 reverses the puck. D1 stays with F1. The second forward, F2, goes in for the puck.

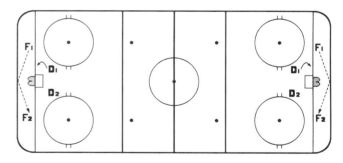

DZ 4

Defensive-zone coverage lead up drill.
F1 passes or skates behind the net. D1 stays with F1 if F1 goes behind the net and if D1 is within half a stick length away from F1. If D1 is not a half stick length away he goes to the front of the net.

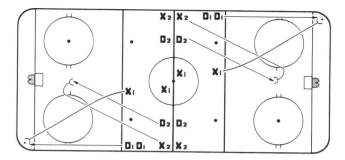

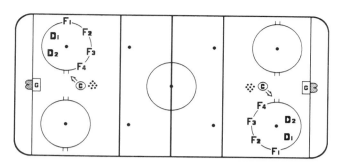

DZ 5

Set up the players as shown. On the whistle, D1 goes after the puck that has been placed in the corner. X1 at the blue line pressures D1. X2 drives to the high slot and D2 must pick up X2.

DZ 7

Man-to-man defensive-zone coverage drill.

The players are on their knees. The coach dumps the puck into the corner. D1, D2, and F1 play defence against F2, F3, and F4. The play must be below the top of the circles.

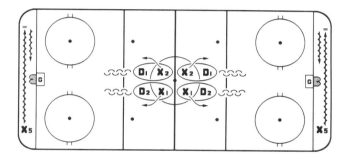

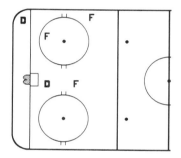

DZ 6

X3 is skating behind the net with a puck. X1 and X2 attack D1 and D2 who play man-on-man coverage. X1 and X2 must try to escape the checking pressure of D1 and D2 to receive a pass from X3 below the goal line.

Variation: Use three-on-three, with X5 the low player.

DZ 8

Defensive positioning with no opposition.

The coach can describe a particular puck location (e.g., in the right corner) and the players must react and position themselves defensively on the coach's command.

Variation: The coach can point his stick to a particular puck position (e.g., behind the net).

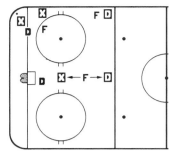

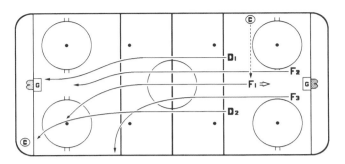

DZ 9

The five defenders play without sticks against five offensive players with sticks.

Variation: Play five-on-five with the defensive players turning their sticks upside-down or play with sticks with the blades cut off before the heel (use broken sticks to cut off).

DZ 12

The players break out five-on-none and make a play on goal. The coach gives a pass to the high man for a second shot. The coach then blows the whistle and five players return to the defensive-zone coverage with another coach acting as the offensive puck position (i.e. in the corner, behind the net etc.).

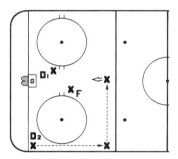

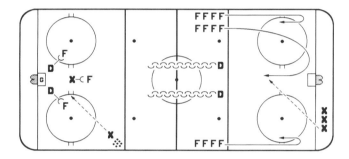

DZ 10

Position players as shown. The puck starts in the corner and is passed as indicated with a shot on goal. D1, D2, and F must defend on the three low opposition players.

DZ 13

The three forwards F break out on the two defencemen D with X being the backchecker after making a breakout pass. The two Ds must read the rush. In the defensive zone, the play becomes a three-on-three. After the play is completed, the coach passes a puck to F and a three-on-three begins again.

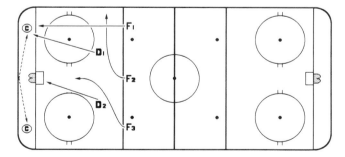

DZ 11

The coach shoots a puck in. The five players break out five-on-zero then leave the puck and go into defensive-zone coverage reacting to the two coaches in the corners moving the puck back and forth.

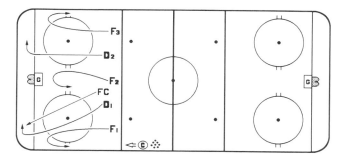

DZ 14

The coach shoots the puck in the corner and the three **F** and two **D** break out with the forechecker **FC** attempting to break up the play.

Variation: Use two, then three forecheckers.

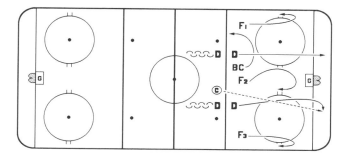

DZ 15

The coach shoots the puck in the corner and the three **F** and two **D** break out with one backchecker **BC** curling inside the blue line to pick up a forward in the lane.

Variation: Five-on-two breakout with two backcheckers.

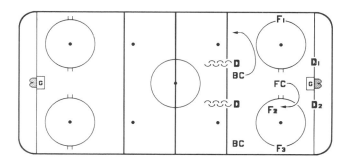

DZ 16

The three **F** and two **D** break out with one fore-checker **FC** and one backchecker **BC** in opposition. The backcheckers move into the defensive zone.

Variation: Five-on-two breakout with one forechecker, one backchecker, and one late backchecker (positioned on the side boards at the blue line). The backcheckers move into the defensive zone and go five-on-five.

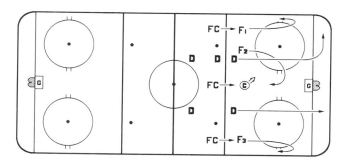

DZ 17

The coach shoots the puck into the zone. Three forecheckers (**FC**) forecheck and play five-on-five. The play ends when the defensive team breaks out over the blue line.

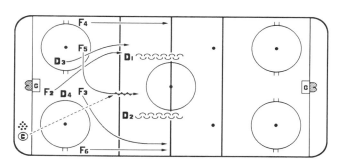

DZ 18

F2 and **F3** from the previous attack backcheck to support **D1** and **D2** against **F4**, **F5**, and **F6**, making the drill a five-on-four. **D1** and **D2** must read the rush to determine who is covering each player defensively.

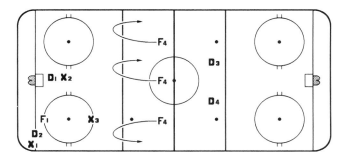 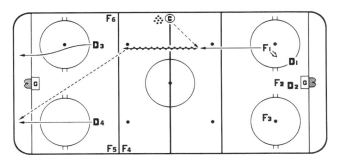

DZ 19

On the whistle, X1, X2, and X3 start the drill. They go three-on-three with D1, D2, and F1. On the second whistle, the first group passes to one of the F4, who go three-on-two on D3 and D4. The high player X3 now backchecks to make the drill a three-on-three.

DZ 20

After a five-on-two play on goal coming from a breakout, the forwards leave the zone. The coach passes a puck to one forward. The forward shoots the puck in for the next five players, who break out and go five-on-two. The player who shoots the puck in becomes either a forechecker or a backchecker on the group breaking out. This is a continuous drill.

Variation: The two forwards who don't get the puck from the coach either forecheck or backcheck on the next break out. The player who shoots the puck moves to the side boards out of the play.

19
Forwards: Offensive Zone

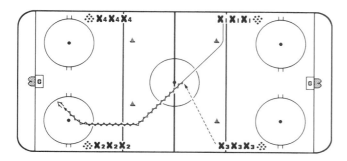

OZ 1

Set up the players as shown. X1 skates through the neutral-zone circle receiving a pass from X3 and drives to the net for a shot on goal. X2 receives a pass from X4, etc. The players stay at the opposite end.

Variation: X1 and X2 start at the same time.

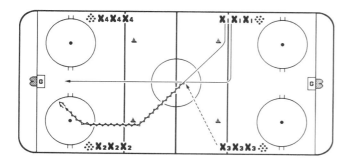

OZ 2

Set up the drill as shown. This is the same as the previous drill except two players go. The puck carrier shoots or passes the puck to his partner driving to the net for a tip-in or rebound. Players change sides after shooting.

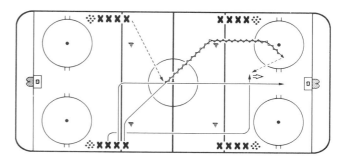

OZ 3

Set the drill up as shown. This drill is the same as the two previous drills but in this drill three players go. The puck carrier goes wide and deep, the second player drives for the net, and the third curls behind the pylon and becomes a trailer (support) for the puck carrier, who passes the puck back to the trailer for the shot on goal.

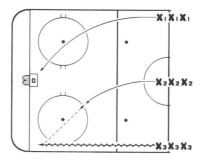

OZ 4

X3 carries the puck wide and deep while X1 drives to the far post. X2 supports X3 by coming over to the puck side of center to receive a pass from X3. X2 can shoot, pass back to X3, or pass to X1. The players change lines after each three-on-zero.

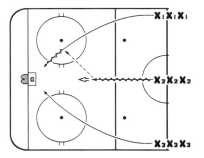

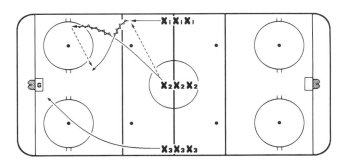

OZ 5

X2 brings the puck over the blue line and stops, or slows, or moves laterally. X1 and X3 drive to the goal for a pass or a rebound if X2 shoots.

OZ 8

X2 passes the puck to X1 and then cuts across as the trailer. X1 leaves a drop pass for X2. X3 and X1 skate hard to the goal. X2 passes back to X1 for a shot on goal.

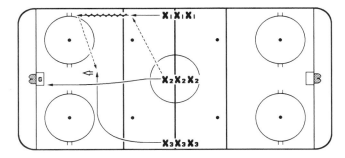

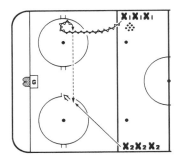

OZ 6

X2 passes to X1 then drives to the goal simulating a pick-off of the off-side defender. X3 comes in late as the high forward for a shot on goal.

OZ 9

X1 carries the puck into the zone wide and deep and delays by curling. X2 starts as X1 does his delay and drives for the net, taking the pass from X1 and then shooting on goal.

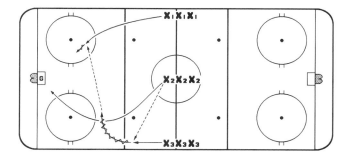

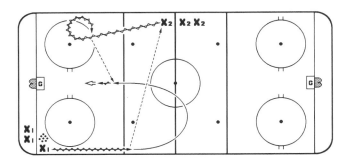

OZ 7

X2 passes to X3, then cuts in behind X3, and drives to the goal. X3 passes to X1 skating down the far side.

OZ 10

Position players as shown. X1 skates up the boards with a puck and upon reaching the blue line passes rink-wide to X2. X2 skates into the zone, does a delay (curl) at the hash marks, and passes to X1, who has cut across-ice and down the slot. Both ends go at the same time.

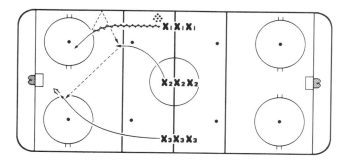

OZ 11

X1 after crossing the blue line bank-passes back to the support trailer X2. X2 retrieves the puck and passes quickly to X3, who is breaking for the net.

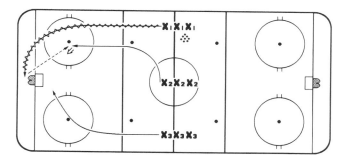

OZ 12

X1 carries the puck in and does a pass back from behind the net on the same side to X2, who is in a support position. X2 shoots with X3 driving to the net for a rebound.

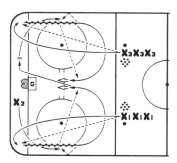

OZ 13

Cycling (quiet zone). X1 starts by making a soft pass to the corner. X1 skates in quickly to retrieve the puck and heads up the ice. X1 board-passes back to X2 who now moves up behind X1. X1 goes to the high slot and receives a pass from X2 for a shot on goal. X2 skates below the goal line for drill on the opposite side.

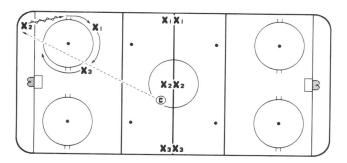

OZ 14

Cycling (quiet zone). The coach shoots the puck into the corner. X1, X2, and X3 skate the circle, back-passing the puck off the boards into the corner. After three back-passes, the low player passes to the player in the slot for a shot on goal.

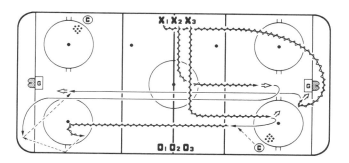

OZ 15

X1, X2, and X3 all go on the whistle. After the shot, X3 receives a pass from the coach and drives wide and deep to the opposite end. X2 follows the play up the ice. X3 delays (curls) and cycles (back board passes) the puck low. X2 follows up and picks up the puck in the corner. X1 looks for a pass from X2 and takes a shot on goal. At the same time that the X players are going, so do the O players from the other side of the ice.

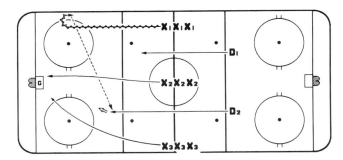

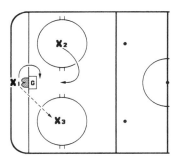

OZ 16

X1 comes into the zone, delays (curls), and passes to the far side D2. D2 shoots with X3 and X2 going to the net.

OZ 19

With X1 behind the goal, X2 and X3 are on the face-off dots. If X1 passes to X3, then X2 moves to the slot for a rebound or is support for X3. X1 comes out the opposite side for a shot or rebound.

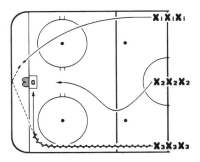

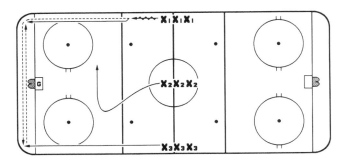

OZ 17

X3 brings the puck in deep and board-passes to X1 supporting behind the goal. X3 and X2 go to the goal for picks, screens, etc. X1 can try to stuff, pass to X2 or X3.

OZ 20

X1 shoots the puck in hard around the boards or glass. X3 races to the corner to get the puck and immediately passes back behind the goal to X1. X3 passes to X2 in the high slot for a shot on goal.

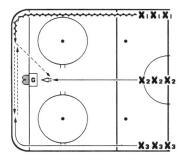

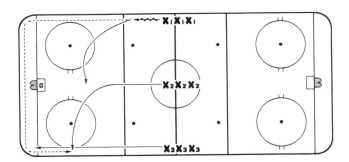

OZ 18

X1 from one side skates in behind the goal line and passes the puck behind the net to X3 coming from the other side of the ice. The pass is returned and passed out to X2, who shoots a quick shot from the slot.

OZ 21

X1 shoots the puck in hard around the boards or glass. X3 skates hard to the corner but lets the puck go to X2 (late forward). X2 can pass to X3 down low or feed a pass to X1.

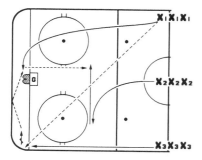

OZ 22

X1 dumps the puck into the opposite corner. X3 board-passes to X1 behind the net. X1 quick passes to X2 in the slot for a shot.

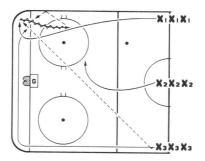

OZ 23

X3 does a diagonal shoot-in. X1 retrieves the puck and turns up the boards but backboard passes (cycles) the puck back to X2, who followed the pass to provide support for the shoot-in.

20
Defencemen

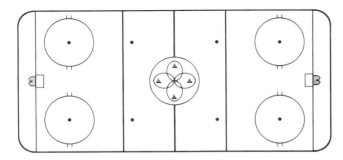

D 1

Players skate figure "8"s around the pylons backward, with or without pucks.

D 2

Position Ds in four different areas of the ice.
(1) Ds skate backward, opening up every other stride and a different way (left or right) each time.
(2) Skate the circle one-quarter forward, one-quarter backward, one-quarter forward, and finally one-quarter backward. Pivot a different way each time.
(3) Skate a figure "8" backward.
(4) Skate a figure "8" backward and forward, pivoting at the top and bottom of the "8."

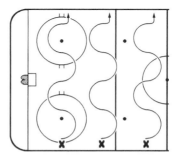

D 3

Players move in a wave across the ice, making three to four crossovers each way.

Variation: The same exercise but change the direction in response to a signal and do it going the length of the ice.

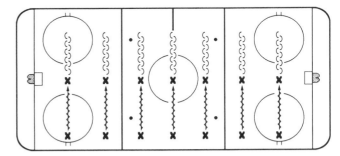

D 4

One player moves forward, the other backward across the ice. The puck is passed back and forth using different skills, such as flipping the puck and batting it down with a glove, one-touch passing, etc.

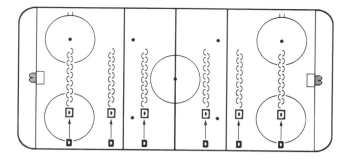

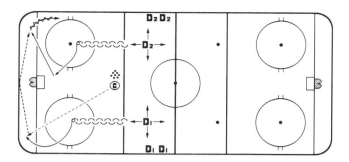

D 5

The players are paired off. The attacking players skate forward using three to four crossovers. The defenders skate backward attempting to stay in front.

Variation: The attackers use a puck but the defenders do not aggressively attempt to check it away.

D 8

D1 and D2 do agility skating in the neutral zone and skate backward to the face-off dot. The coach shoots a puck into the corner. D1 picks up the puck and board-passes to D2, who skates quickly to the blue line.

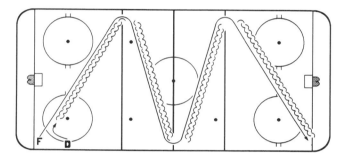

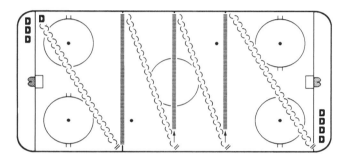

D 6

F skates the pattern as shown. D skates the pattern backward always trying to maintain position on F.

D 9

The players skate backward to each of the lines and then do stepovers across the width of the ice on the lines.

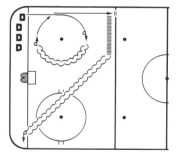

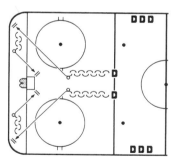

D 7

The Ds are in the corner. One at a time, they skate the circle, always facing the far end of the ice. On reaching the blue line, they stop, do stepovers to the middle of the ice, then skate backward to the opposite corner. The next player goes when the one ahead passes upon completing the circle. After all the players have gone, they go the other way.

D 10

The players skate backward from the blue line and at a pylon or signal, turn to the outside and skate forward to the corner and stop. They then skate backward a few strides, turn in the opposite direction to their first turn, and skate to the net and stop. Switch sides after each time through the drill.

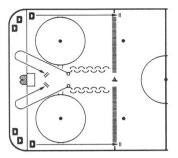

D 11

The players skate forward from the goal line to the blue line, do stepovers halfway across the blue line, skate backward to the hash marks, turn to the outside, and skate deep into the corner. They then make a sharp turn and return to the front of the net.

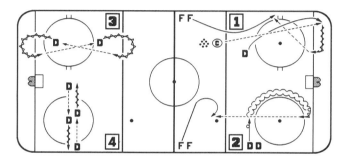

D 12

Position players in four groups around the ice as shown.

(1) The coach shoots a puck in the corner. D skates in, retrieves the puck, starts up-ice, and passes to F, who skated to a breakout spot on the hash marks.

(2) D skates to the top of the face-off circle, pivots, and skates backward for half the circle. At bottom of the circle, D passes to F, who is on the move.

(3) Ds skate figure "8" patterns and pass each other a puck as they come out of their tight turns.

(4) Both Ds skate towards the boards. As front D approaches the boards, the one trailing passes the puck. On receiving puck, both players tight-turn and repeat the action going the other way.

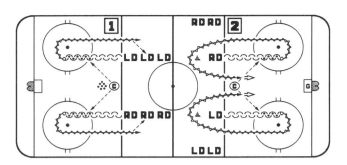

D 13

(1) D receives a pass from the coach while skating backward. D skates around the dot (or pylon) and skates forward, passing to the D next in line for a shot.

(2) After D skates out around the pylon in the neutral zone, D races back to the goal for a shot.

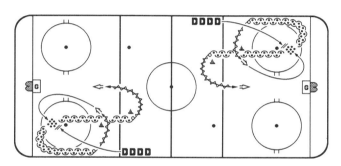

D 14

D skates into the circle, picks up a puck, pivots backward, and skates backward to the corner. D1 continues to skate backward up the boards, pivots, skates forward around the pylon, and takes a shot on goal. After the shot, D skates back into the circle, picks up a puck, and skates backward to the pylon outside the blue line, pivots, and skates back into the zone for a second shot on goal.

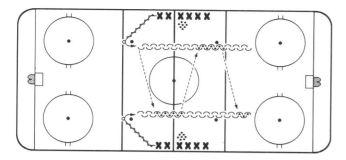

D 15

The front player in each line (the one with the puck) skates to mid-ice and passes the puck to his partner. Both skate backward to the goal line, passing the puck between them.

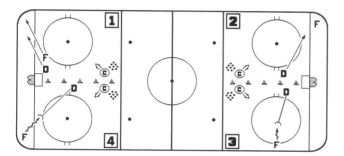

D 16

Divide the ice into zones with pylons as indicated.
(1) A coach spots a puck. F retrieves the puck and D must decide to pressure or contain.
(2) A coach passes to F. D plays one-on-one from the corner.
(3) D meets F at the hash marks and tries to check or contain F.
(4) D meets F and tries to check or angle F.

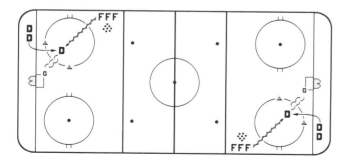

D 17

F tries to get by D whose area is between the two pylons. F must get past D before taking a shot on goal.

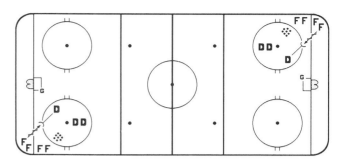

D 18

This is a similar drill to the previous one, only F comes out of the corner. D must use good agility skating and proper angling. Use the pylons to confine the space.

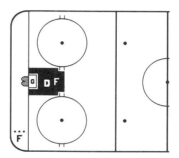

D 19

The player in the corner has three pucks and passes them out to the forward in the low slot. The forward must move around the low slot area and get open for a pass and shot on goal. D practices controlling the player in a legal manner by angling, blocking, pushing, or using his stick. You can use defencemen as forwards for this drill and rotate.

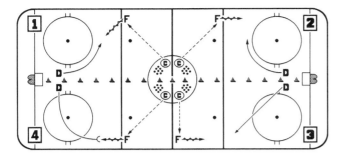

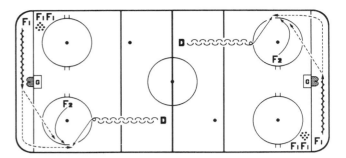

D 20

Divide the ice into zones with pylons as indicated.
(1) D angles F from the inside/out. F stays on the boards.
(2) Offensive player has choice of direction to the goal. D must defend against that choice.
(3) D reads the pressure, contains F, and checks on the boards.
(4) D plays one-on-one from the blue line.

D 22

F1 skates behind the goal and passes the puck around the boards. F2 and D read the play and D must decide to pinch or retreat and play one-on-one with F2.

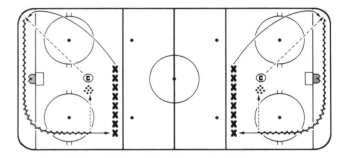

D 21

Divide the ice into zones 1, 2, 3, and 4 with pylons as shown. A coach shoots the puck into the corner from the blue line, zones 2 and 3, or down low, zones 1 and 4. Two players go for the puck. The player with the puck becomes offence and the other player becomes defence.

D 23

The coach shoots a puck in the corner. D skates into the corner looking over his shoulder with his head on a swivel. D gets the puck, carries it behind the net, and up the far boards before passing it back to the coach.

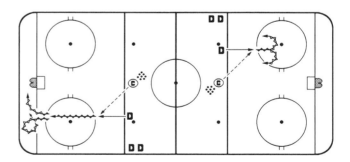

D 24

D skates in and takes a pass from the coach. In one situation, D immediately does a tight turn after receiving the puck. In the other situation, D has carried the puck deep into the zone and can go directly behind the net or do a tight turn to avoid a check and then go behind the net. The coach can indicate which way to turn.

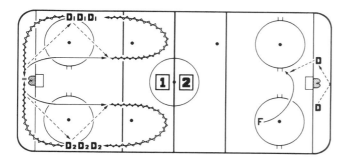

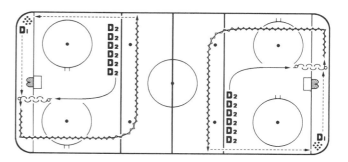

D 25

(1) D1 carries the puck behind the goal, stops to read the forechecking, and passes back to the next D1 for a give-and-go breakout play.
(2) D1 passes to D2 behind the net using a board pass. D2 passes to the curling forward.

D 28

With D1 in the corner, D2 comes down toward the slot, pivots, and skates backward to the boards to receive an outlet pass/option from the corner. D2 rushes the puck up the boards and across the ice to the back of the line.

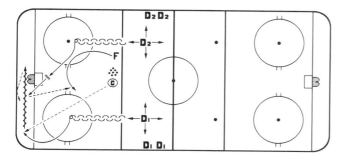

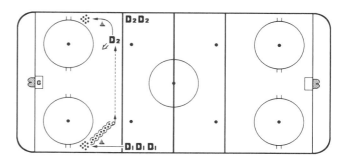

D 26

Defence reverse to defence.
D2 goes to the front of the goal. D1 carries the puck behind the goal and reverses the puck to D1. D2 passes to a curling F.

D 29

D1 skates forward, picks up a puck, pivots, and skates backward to the blue line. D1 then passes to D2, who shoots and then does the same sequence as D1.

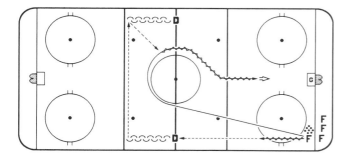

D 27

F starts out with the puck and passes to the D on his side. D skates backward with the puck and passes it to his defence partner, who then gives F a pass as he curls around the center circle.

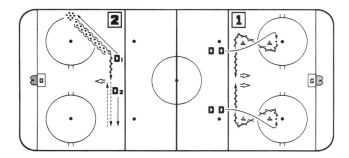 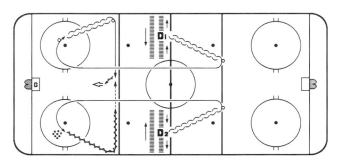

D 30

(1) Place the pylons and pucks as shown. D skates figure "8" forward and backward, finishing with a shot on goal while still in motion. D on other side then goes. Switch sides.

(2) The Ds start at the same time. D1 skates to the hash marks, retrieves a puck, and skates backward to the starting spot. D1 pivots and passes to D2, who has skated towards the boards. D2 takes the pass and returns it to D1, who takes a shot on goal. Players switch positions.

D 32

D1 and D2 start the drill at the center red line as shown. They do stepovers to the boards, back to the edge of the center-ice face-off circle, and then back to where they started. They then pivot and skate backward (45-degree angle) to the blue line, pivot, and drive for the face-off dot in the far end. After doing a tight turn around the face-off dot, D2 picks up a puck, skates to the blue line, and cuts across the ice, giving a pass to D1 cutting across the ice. D1 takes a shot on goal while D2 drives to the net for a rebound. Change sides after each turn.

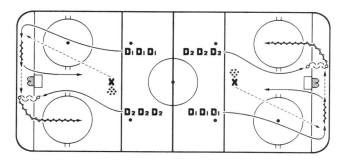

D 31

The coach shoots the puck into the corner. D1 or D2 from the blue line retrieves the puck in the corner. D1 passes to D2 and they both skate to the center-ice area, passing to each other.

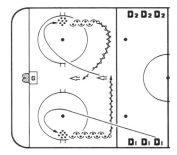

D 33

Position the players as shown. D1 skates in and does a tight turn around the face-off dot. After picking up a puck, D1 skates to the blue line, cuts across the ice, and takes a shot on goal as he reaches the middle of the ice. D1 then goes to pick up another puck in the other face-off circle, cuts across ice, and takes a shot on goal after entering the slot area.

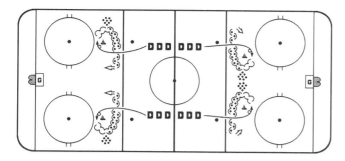 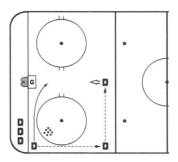

D 34

In one end, the D players skate inside-out, pick up a puck, and skate laterally to the middle and shoot. At the other end of the ice, Ds skate outside-in and shoot from the board side of the pylon.

D 36

The D in the corner passes to the D in different ways – off the boards, off the glass, bouncing, etc. D then goes to the net for deflections. D quickly passes to his partner on the blue line, who then takes a shot on goal.

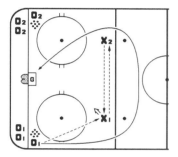

D 35

Position the players as shown. D1 passes to X1 and X1 passes to X2. X2 returns the pass to X1, who takes a shot on goal. After passing the puck, D1 skates out around the neutral-zone face-off dots and then drives for the net looking for deflection and/or rebounds from the shot of X1. This drill can be done in both ends of the ice at the same time.

21

Goaltending

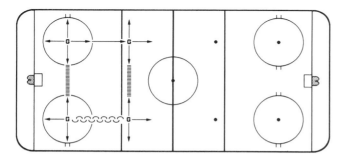

G 1

The goaltender moves in and out and side to side at each dot, backward and forward to the goal, and side-shuffles across ice to the next dot.

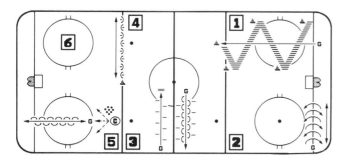

G 2

(1) Zig-zag backward, stopping at the pylons.
(2) One foot hops over the goal line.
(3) Knee drops. Skating forward, skating backward.
(4) Cariokas. Cross right skate over left skate, then right skate behind left skate, etc.
(5) Skate forward, backward, react to thrown puck.
(6) Drop and recover. Knees, stomach, rear, back.
   Variation: Stop a puck on recovery.

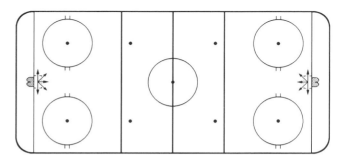

G 3

The goaltender moves from side to side and in and out, returning to the middle each time.

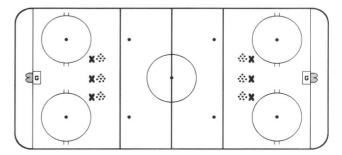

G 4

All the players shoot their own pucks, one at a time, before going to the next player. They shoot at the catcher, then the blocker, then the right skate and left skate, and finally at the pads. The player goes in for the rebound on the final shot.

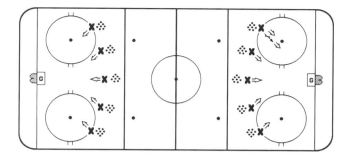

G 5

The players shoot going across the semi-circle or alternate side to side.

Variation: Each player has two pucks. The first puck is shot, then the player skates in for a shot with the second puck.

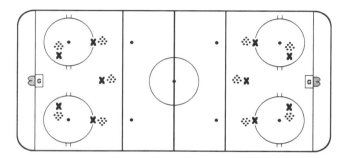

G 6

Players shoot from various angles on a signal from the coach.

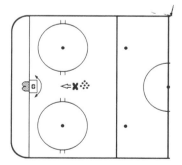

G 7

The goaltender holds one post and the shooter shoots for the opposite side. The goaltender must move across. Shots should be low and high.

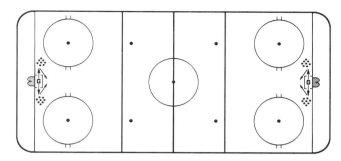

G 8

Pucks are placed on each side of the crease. The goaltender, without a stick, moves from the middle of the crease, picks up a puck, returns and places it in the middle of the crease. Move side to side.

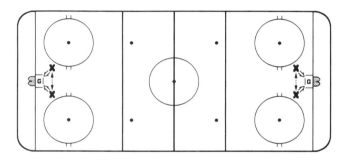

G 9

The player passes the puck across the crease. The goaltender does a double-pad save. Sometimes, the passer will shoot so the goaltender does not cheat on the drill.

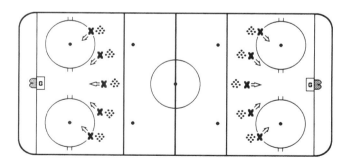

G 10

The goaltender is down on one knee. Players shoot as the goaltender recovers to a proper stance. Players can slap their sticks on the ice for the signal for the goaltender to recover. Shoot as the goaltender regains his stance.

Variations: Goaltender is down on both knees, on stomach, facing the shooters, or is facing the end boards.

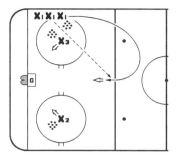

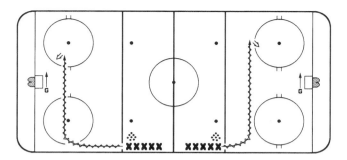

G 11

Position players as shown. X1 skates around the face-off dot (or pylon) and receives a pass from line X1. X1 shoots a slap shot or snap shot on goal from the blue line. X2 shoots a snap shot as soon as the first shot hits the goaltender. X3 shoots a wrist shot as soon as the second shot hits the goaltender. X1 goes to X2, X2 goes to X3, and X3 goes to the X1 line.

G 14

Players skate in from the boards and across the top of the face-off circles. The goaltender moves across the crease with the shooter. The shooter can shoot at any time.

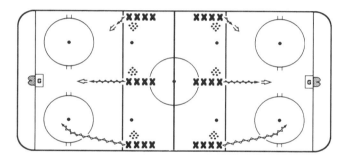

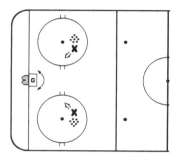

G 12

Place players as shown. Three players shoot with three seconds between each shot. The first player shoots inside the blue line, the second from the high slot and the third pulls the goaltender.

G 15

Two players alternate shooting from the circles. The goaltender tries to stop the puck with and without a stick.

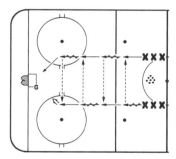

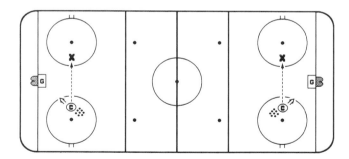

G 13

The two players pass the puck to each other and shoot on goal.

G 16

The coach either shoots or passes across for the shot. The goaltender reacts to the shot or the pass and then prepares for the next shot.

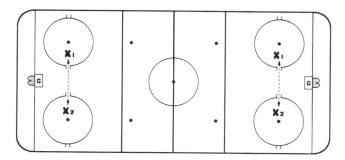

G 17

X1 and X2 pass back and forth with the goaltender moving with the pass. X1 or X2 finally shoot.

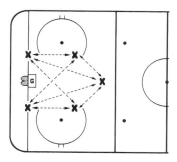

G 18

The players pass to each other and then the last player touching the puck takes a shot on goal.

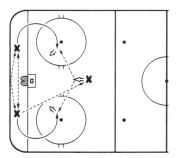

G 19

The players pass the puck to each other behind the goal and then pass to X in the high slot. The player in the slot can shoot or pass to one of the players down low, who now are in position off each post.

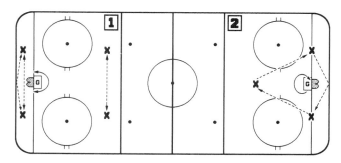

G 20

(1) The players pass the puck at the blue line or behind the net. The goalie must move accordingly to the position of the puck.

(2) The players pass behind the net and to the player in the slot. The goaltender sets up accordingly.

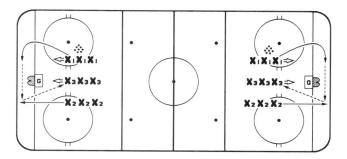

G 21

X1 shoots the puck off the glass, retrieves, it and passes to X2, who passes to X3 for the shot. X1 can also pass to X3 or come out from behind the goal.

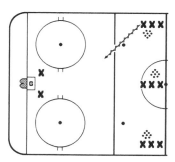

G 22

The players from the three lines shoot and the two players in front try to deflect the puck or screen the goaltender.

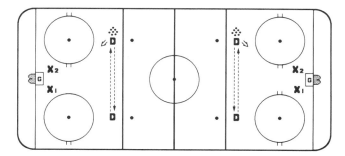

G 23

The Ds pass the puck back and forth and then shoot. X1 and X2 screen and/or deflect.

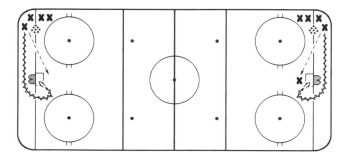

G 24

The player in the corner passes the first puck across the crease and attempts to pass or come out in front with the second puck.

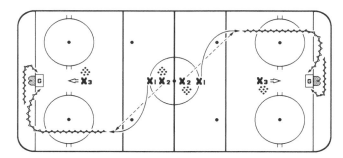

G 25

Position players as shown. X1 skates wide and takes a pass from X2 at the blue line. X1 then skates in on the short side and tries to jam the puck or go behind the net to try a wraparound. After X1 has taken the shot, the goaltender must quickly recover to handle a shot from X3.

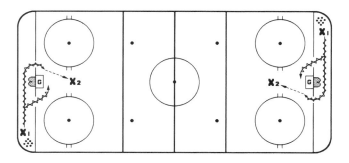

G 26

X1 comes out from the corner for a shot or pass to X2 for a shot. X1 can also go behind the goal, passing to X2 as X1 comes out the other side of the goal.

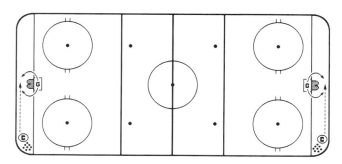

G 27

The goaltender moves side to side, in and out, and stops a puck behind the goal from one side then the other.

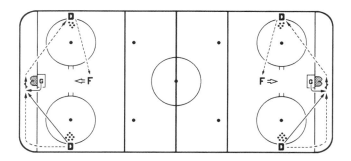

G 28

D rims the puck. D passes to D, who passes to F, who shoots. The goaltender must stop the puck behind the goal and leave it there for D before returning quickly to the goal to get ready for the next shot.

22
Evaluation

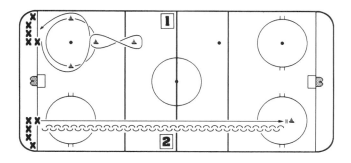

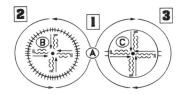

E 1 (Skate 30)

(1) The player skates around the circle into a small figure "8" and completes the circle. Time the player.
(2) The player skates forward down the ice to the face-off dot (pylon), stops, and skates backward to the red line. Time the player.

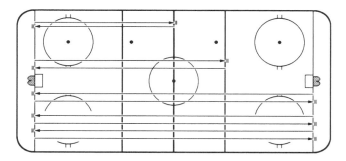

E 2

The players skate for speed at five distances:
(1) Center red line and back.
(2) Far blue line and back.
(3) Far boards (one length).
(4) Far boards and back (two lengths).
(5) Far boards and back, twice (four lengths).

E 3

(1) Skate a figure "8" backwards.
(2) Start in the middle, skate backward to the circle, crossovers for one-quarter circle and forward to the dot. Repeat as many times as you can in time allowed.
(3) Start in the middle. Skate backward to the circle and forward to the dot. Repeat as many times as you can in time allowed.
(4) Start in the middle. Skate forward to the circle, pivot, skate backward one-quarter circle, and then do stepovers back to the dot. Repeat as many times as you can in time allowed.

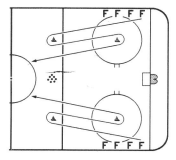

E 4

The forwards start in opposite corners, skate around the pylons, and race for the puck. The first player to the puck takes a shot on goal while the other player tries to prevent it.

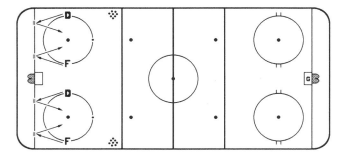

E 5

D and F start on the inside hash marks at the same time. They sprint to the goal line, stop, and then race for the puck at the top of the circle. The winner drives for the net while the other player is the back-checker applying pressure.

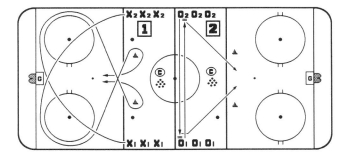

E 6

(1) X1 and X2 skate the circle, skate for the pylon, and do an outside-in turn and race for the puck.
(2) O1 and O2 skate hard to the opposite side boards, touch the boards with their sticks, and race for the puck.

In both drills, the first player tries to score while the second player tries to prevent a goal.

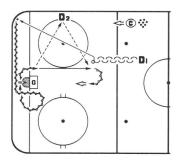

E 7

A puck is shot into a corner. D1 skates backward, pivots (a pylon can designate where to pivot), and skates to the corner. D1 gets the puck while doing a head-and-shoulder fake, skates behind the net and toward the far face-off circle. Coming out, D1 does a tight turn and returns behind the net. After stopping, D1 then starts again and passes to D2 near the boards. D1 skates out in front for the return pass from D2, does another tight turn, and shoots on goal. D1 then skates to D2's position on the boards and D2 goes to the blue line to repeat the drill.

E 8

The coach shoots a puck into the corner and the two players race for the puck and attempt to score. The play continues until the coach blows the whistle, a goal is scored, or the goaltender freezes the puck.

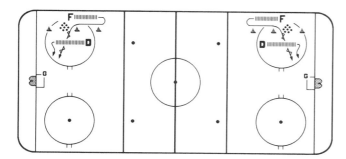 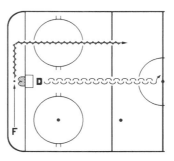

E 9

Place three pylons so that D has to do crossovers further than F. On the whistle, both players move towards the goal. F returns, picks up a puck, and goes one-on-one with D after the crossovers.

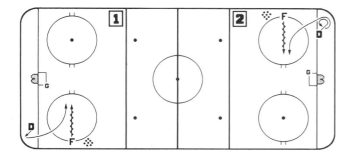

E 10

(1) F starts at the hash marks on the boards and D starts in the corner. F tries to get a shot on goal and D tries to prevent it.
(2) D is facing the boards and does a 360-degree turn before trying to stop F from getting a shot on goal.

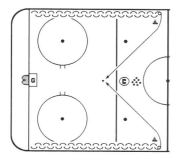

E 11

Position D as shown. The front player in each line skates backward around the pylon, pivots, and races for the puck. The player with the puck tries to score. The other player tries to check D with the puck.

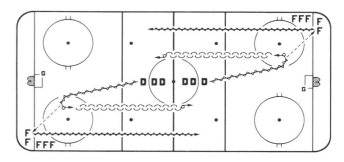

E 12

F starts from the corner, skates behind the net, and picks up a puck. F then skates down the ice between the face-off dots and the boards. As soon as F touches the puck, D starts skating backward without turning until he reaches the center red line. D then turns and tries to ride F out to the boards, while F attempts to cut in and score.

NOTE: D starts this drill halfway between the top of the goal crease and the hash marks of the face-off circles.

E 13

D skates to the inside hash marks, passes to F in the corner, and skates backward to the red line before being allowed to turn to play F, who is carrying the puck.

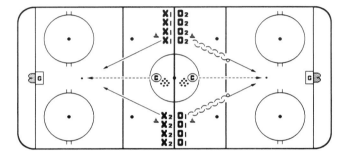

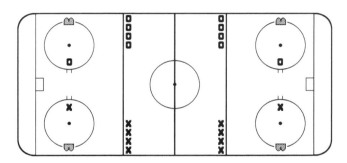

E 14

The coaches place pucks as shown and O1 and O2 at one end and X1 and X2 at the other end race for it.

Variation: Players skate backward to the blue line, pivot, and race for the puck.

E 17

Players cross the ice one-on-one, as the coach blows the whistle every 30 to 45 seconds. The players leave the puck, clear the zone, and two new players start.

Variation: Two-on-two or three-on-three.

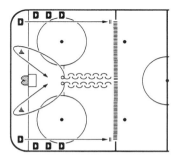

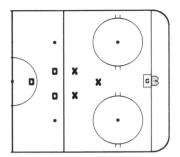

E 15

The front player in each line skates from the goal line to the blue line, cross-steps halfway across the blue line, skates backward to the hash marks of the circle, pivots to the outside, and skates to the corner. The player makes a sharp turn and returns to the front of the net.

E 18

The players play three-on-three on the entire ice surface or in two halves. Rotate the players and change every minute. The players change on the fly with a whistle and the team with the puck on the change passes back to their own goaltender.

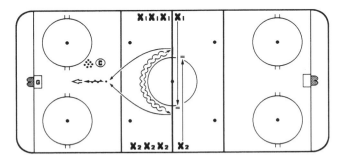

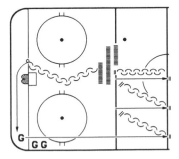

E 16

X1 and X2 start at the same time. They each skate to the furthest edge of the center-ice circle, stop, backward skate around half the circle, and when they reach the center red line they race for the puck set up inside the blue line.

E 19

The goaltenders skate backward, forward, backward and sideways, stop, and shuffle-step right and left as shown.

23
Conditioning

The specific on-ice conditioning drills in this chapter are designed to train the three energy systems and to be incorporated into a practice. Suggestions for work-to-rest ratios and repetitions are:

ANAEROBIC ALACTIC SYSTEM
(short intense work)

Drills 1 to 5
5 to 15 seconds
Work-to-rest ratio 1:6 to 1:5
5 repetitions equal 1 set
Build to 4 sets, i.e., 20 repetitions
Use four to five groups. One group works while the others rest.

Allow for a longer rest/relief period after each set.

ANAEROBIC LACTIC SYSTEM
(medium intense work)

Drills 6 to 30
30 to 60 seconds
Work-to-rest ratio 1:5 to 1:3
4 repetitions equal 1 set
Build to three sets, i.e., 12 repetitions
Use three or four groups. One group works while the others rest.

Allow for a longer rest/relief period after each set.

AEROBIC SYSTEM
(long moderate work)

Drills 31 to 33
3 minutes or longer work
Work-to-rest ratio 2:1 to 1:2
Build to 20 minutes of continuous skating

NOTE: It is now recommended that players skate easy every three minutes and stretch the back for 10 seconds to prevent or alleviate back pain.

TRAINING THE ANAEROBIC ALACTIC SYSTEM
Drills 1 to 5

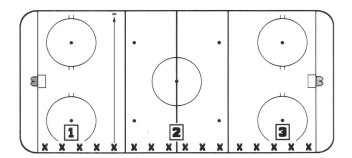

CO 1
Each of the three groups skates one width of the ice or from the goal line to the center red line, in turn.

Variation: Each of the three groups skates two widths of the ice or from the goal line to the center red line and back, in turn.

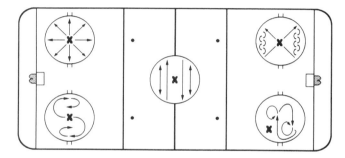

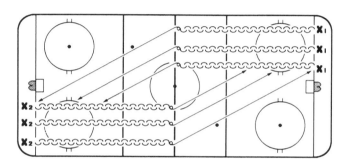

CO 2

The players perform a different drill in each circle – stops and starts, figure "8"s, speed around the circle, etc.

CO 5

X1 and X2 players skate backward to the center red line, pivot and skate diagonally across the ice to the far corner.

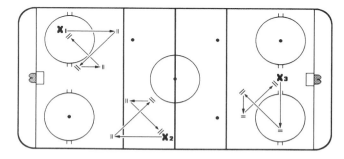

TRAINING THE ANAEROBIC LACTIC SYSTEM
Drills 6 to 30

CO 3

Players skate the preset pattern shown as fast as they can. Run two players at a time then switch to a new set of two.

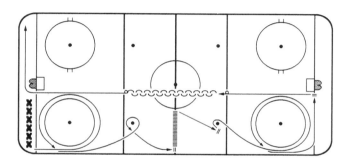

CO 6

Players line up in the corner of the ice. Skate around the circle clockwise (counter-clockwise the second time through), skate to the near neutral-zone dot and do a tight turn, skate forward to the center-ice red line, stop, and do stepovers to the edge of the center-ice face-off circle. The players then skate to the far neutral-zone dot, stop, do a tight turn, and skate around the far face-off circle, clockwise. The players skate to the goal crease, skate hard to the blue line, pivot, skate backward to the other blue line, pivot, and finally skate forward to the other end and go to the far corner.

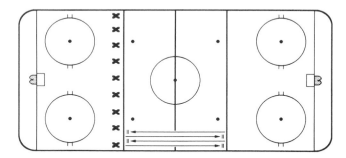

CO 4

Have each group skate blue line to blue line, two, three or four in turn.

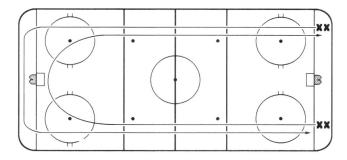

CO 7

The players from one side skate in front of the net and the players from the other side skate behind the net. The players from both sides go at the same time. This can be done with one, two, or three players at one time.

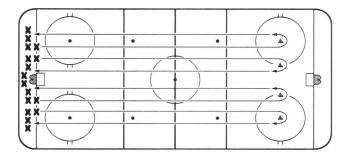

CO 8 (Skate 31)

The player skates down the ice around the pylon and back. The next player in line starts when his partner crosses the goal line.

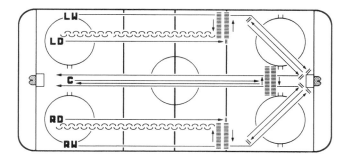

CO 9

All players (one line) go at the same time in this drill. LW and RW skate forward to the far blue line, drive to the net and back twice, and then back to where they started. C skates to the inside hash marks at the far end, does stepovers to the edge of each circle and back to the middle before returning to where the drill started. LD and RD skate to

the far blue line, do stepovers to the boards and back and they skate backward to the goal line where they started.

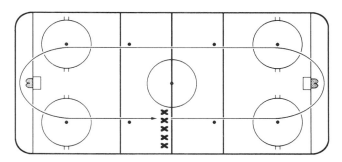

CO 10

Each group skates from two to four laps around the rink.

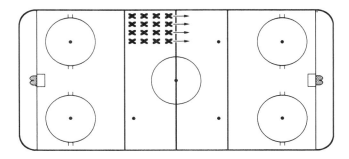

CO 11

The same as previous drill except divide the team into groups and run relay races. Skate two to three laps for each group.

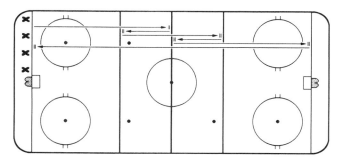

CO 12

Each group skates forward from the goal line to the center red line, back to the near blue line, then to the far blue line, back to the center red line, then go for the far goal line and all the way back.

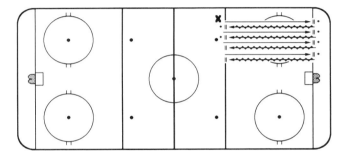

CO 13

Place pucks (five) on the blue line. Players start on the goal line, skate to the blue line, stop, pick up a puck, skate back to the goal line, stop, drop the puck, and repeat until all five pucks have been moved. The second group starts on the blue line and brings five pucks back.

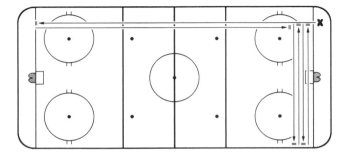

CO 14

The players skate the length of the ice, stop, skate back and then back and forth across the ice twice, and then skate the length of the ice back to starting position.

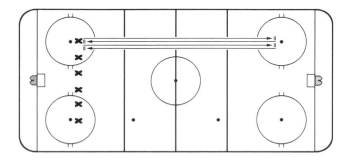

CO 15

Each group skates from the defensive face-off dot to the one at the far end, four times.

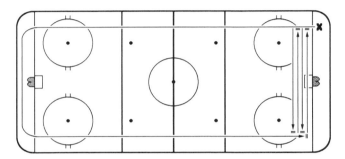

CO 16

The players skate one lap of the ice on the perimeter and skate stepovers across the ice twice.

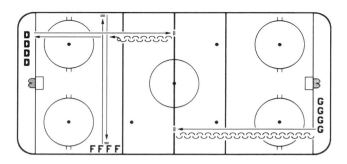

CO 17

Defence: Skate forward to the red line, backward to the blue, and then turn and skate forward to the goal line. Do the drill three times working on backward turns both ways.

Forwards: Skate forward across the rink and back three times, touching the boards with their sticks.

Goaltenders: Skate forward to the center red line, drop to both knees with the goal stick and catcher in the proper position. Then, skate backward to the goal line and do a double leg-pad slide to one side. Do this drill two times but the second time the double leg-pad slide should be to the opposite side of the first one.

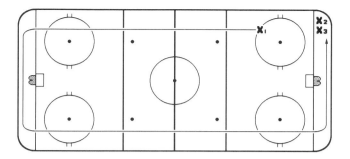

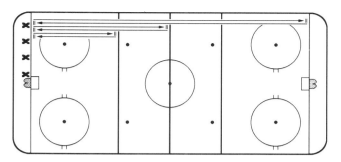

CO 18

Player X1 starts on the top of the circle and three or four players chase X1 around the ice. The chase players start at the bottom of the circle.

CO 21

Each group skates from the near goal line to the far goal line and back, skates to the center red line and back, and skates to the near blue line and back.

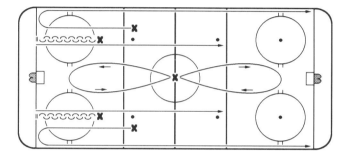

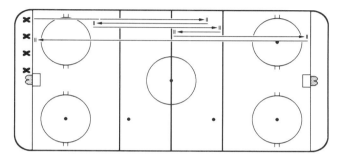

CO 19

Divide the team into five player units. Players practice their breakout system without a puck and at full speed.

CO 22

Each group does stops and starts using the entire length of the ice, changing direction on the whistle. Have the groups work from 20 to 40 seconds.

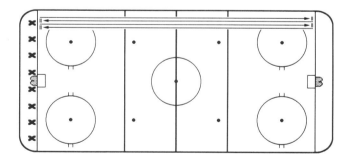

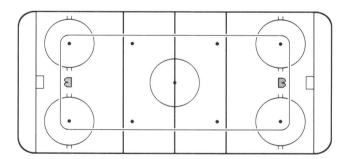

CO 20

Each group skates from goal line to goal line four times.

CO 23

Each group skates around the defensive zone face-off dots for three laps.

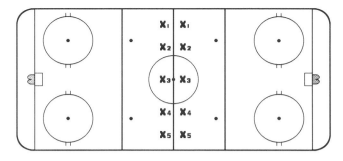

CO 24

Games of one-on-one are played all over the ice. Start at 30 seconds and move up to 90 seconds at a time.

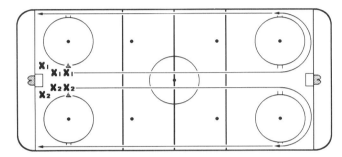

CO 25

X1 and X2 skate the length of the ice, around the face-off circle on their side of the ice and return to the goal line from which they started. The next player goes when the one ahead crosses the goal line.

Variation: Have the players skate hard for one length of the ice and return slowly on the outside. Start again when recovered. Repeat again when recovered. Repeat for five minutes.

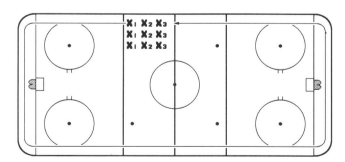

CO 26

The players line up in three groups at the blue line. Each group skates one lap of the ice as hard as they can. The next group goes when the one ahead returns to the starting point.

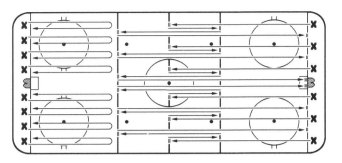

CO 27 (Skate 22)

The players race to the blue line, do tight turns, and then skate back to the goal line. The players then skate to the red line, stop, skate back to the blue line, stop, skate forward to the opposite blue line, stop, and skate to the goal line.

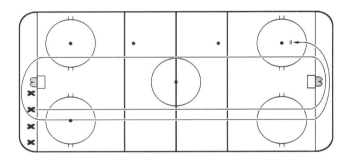

CO 28

Each group skates around the rink behind the nets, one and one-half laps and then goes in the other direction one and one-half laps, in turn.

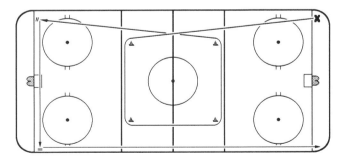

CO 29

The players start in the corner, make a full loop in the neutral zone, skate to the opposite corner and stop, skate the width of the ice, stop and skate to the far end of the ice.

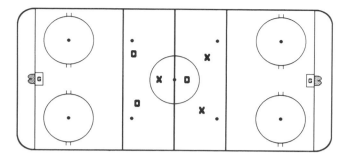

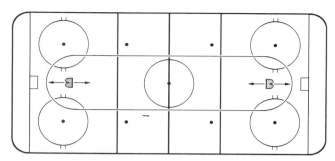

CO 30

Play a three-on-three or a four-on-four scrimmage using the full ice. The players change while the puck is in play. On the change, the puck is passed to the goaltender. On off-sides, the puck is passed back to the goaltender and the offending team must move outside the blue line. The players work for 30 seconds to one minute and then rest. Have the players come in one end of the bench and out the other. The next three or four in order go on the whistle.

CO 32

The players skate around the rink behind the nets but the coaches move the nets towards center ice with each lap. When the nets are at the center face-off circle, have the players skate in the opposite direction and the coaches start moving the nets out again. The drill ends when the nets are back in their starting position.

TRAINING THE AEROBIC SYSTEM
Drills 31 to 33

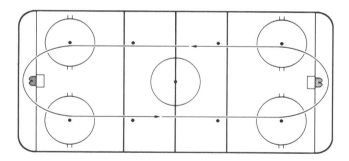

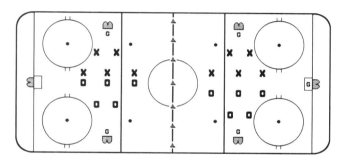

CO 33

The players play two five-on-five scrimmages using half-ice. Each game is 10 minutes in length and change lines after five minutes. The players work for five minutes and rest for five minutes.

CO 31

The entire team skates around the rink going behind each net. The players skate for three minutes and then change direction and skate the other way for another three minutes. Continue the drill for six to fifteen minutes. Move the nets to keep the ice in good condition.

24
Fun Drills

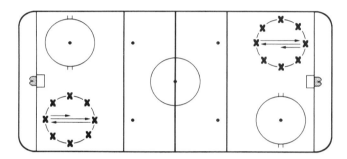

F 1

All the players stand in the circle facing outward (backs to the face-off dot). The "it" player touches another player and sprints back to his vacant spot. If the "it" player is touched before he gets back to his position, this player remains "it."

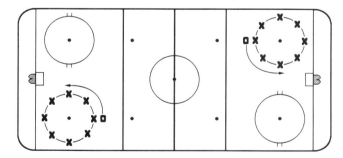

F 2

All players (10 to 12) stand on the perimeter of the circle facing inward. A player designated as "it" skates around the outside and around the perimeter. While moving around the perimeter, the player tags another player who chases the "it" player around the circle. The "it" sprints back to the vacated spot.

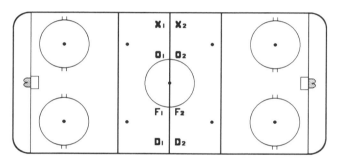

F 3

Multiple pairs are on the ice. Each pair plays a one-on-one game. Winners play against winners.

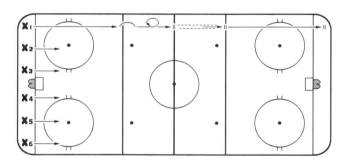

F 4

The players line up in lines behind the goal line for a race. On the whistle, the first players in each line skate full speed to the first blue line, dive on their stomachs, roll over like a log, and then crawl on their hands and knees fast to the far blue line, get up and skate full speed to the goal line at the far end.

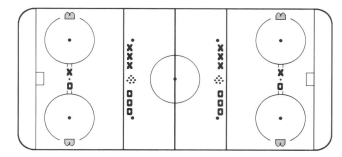

F 5

Place the nets cross-ice in the end zone. All players line up along the appropriate blue line. The coach blows the whistle to start a one-on-one scrimmage between X and O in the zone until one of the players scores. Every 20 seconds thereafter, the coach sends another pair of players.

Variation: Two-on-two and three-on-three.

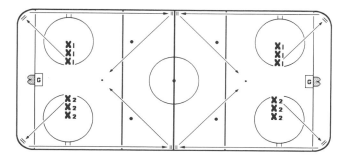

F 6

All four corners start at the same time. Players skate to the corner, stop, skate to the near blue line, stop, and then race for a puck placed at the blue line by the coach. The winner goes in for a shot on goal. The other player can apply pressure or can follow the play for a rebound.

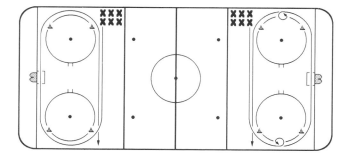

F 7

The players race around the course as shown. Do clockwise and counter-clockwise, forward and backward.

Variation: Players do a 360-degree tight turn at the outside hash marks being sure to turn clockwise at one set of hash marks and counter-clockwise at the marks on the other side.

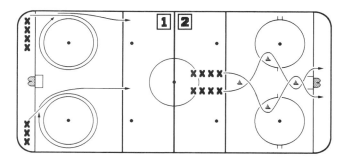

F 8

(1) Circle Race: The players skate the same way around the circle once and finish the race at the blue line. Make sure they race clockwise and counter-clockwise as well as forward and backward.

(2) Diamond Race: Two players skate the course as shown and finish at the goal line. Warn the players to avoid collisions.

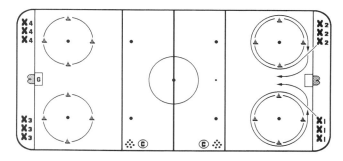

F 9

Position players and pylons as indicated in the diagram. X1 and X2 start the drill by skating the circle counter-clockwise and clockwise respectively. As they come out of the circle, they race for a puck at the blue line (placed there by a coach) with the winner going in for a shot on goal. The other player can apply pressure or can follow the play for a rebound.

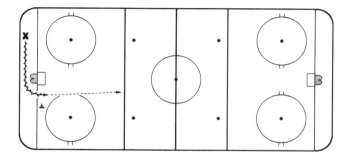

F 10

The players skate around the net and shoot the puck at the empty net at the other end. The puck must be shot before the shooter gets to the hash marks. The game continues until only one player is left.

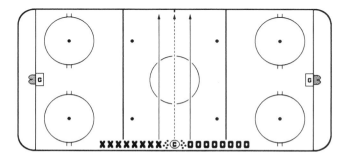

F 11

Divide the team in two. The coach has the pucks at center ice. There will be three separate one-on-one scrimmages at the same time. The coach spots three pucks to create a race between three X and O players. X and O of each contest play until one scores. After a goal is scored, they go back to their bench and the coach will begin the next one-on-one. Since there will be three different groups playing at the same time, tell the players that they can't lift the puck to score unless they are deking. Keep the score by team.

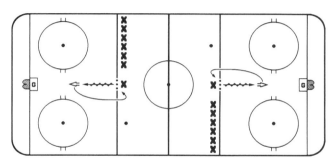

F 12

Place three pucks on the blue line and all players get 20 seconds to try to score with all three pucks. Use both ends of the rink at the same time.

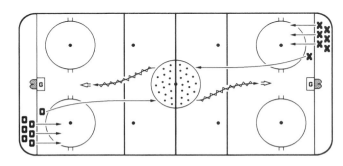

F 13

Pucks are spread out in the center ice circle. On the whistle, each team sprints for the far goal line. On each length, a different player picks up a puck and goes and shoots on the goaltender. The team that scores the most goals and finishes in the least amount of time wins the contest.

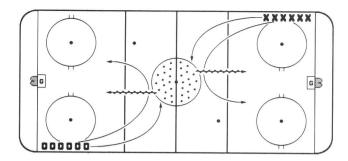

F 14

Divide the players into two teams. Pucks are spread out in the center-ice circle. On the whistle, two players from each team go, pick up a puck, and try to score. They stay on the same puck until they do score. Once they have scored, they go back to center for another puck. The team that gets the most goals in 30 seconds gets one point for their team. The first team to reach seven points wins. (NOTE: Players can't be offside. Goaltenders cannot freeze the puck but must throw it to the corner.)

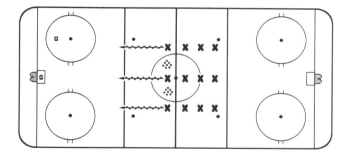

F 15

Form players into groups of three. Three pucks are placed at the center-ice red line. The three players take one puck in and try to score. After scoring, they all return to get another puck to try to score again before going for the final puck. Before any one puck can go in the net, each player must have touched the puck once. Coaches should time groups to determine the winner. Winners leave the ice. Players must try to score all three in 30 seconds. Encourage touch-passing.

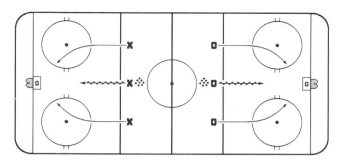

F 16

On the whistle, the three O players and three X players attack their respective goals. Each team tries to score as many goals as possible in 30 seconds. There are no off-sides and all three players must re-enter the zone when retrieving a new puck. They play a puck until they score. The team with the most goals after 30 seconds wins.

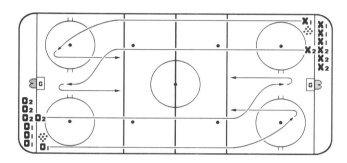

F 17

X1 and X2 and O1 and O2 try to score. They shoot until the puck goes in and then skate hard back to the goal line they came from. The next two then go. The first team to reach 10 goals wins. X1 and X2 and O1 and O2 pass the puck to each other.

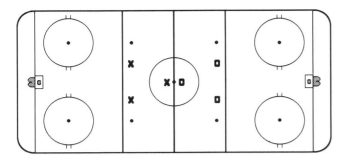

F 18

All players go to the bench. The coach calls out two teams of three. Three pucks are used. A three-on-three starts on the whistle. The game ends when all three pucks are in the net. The next two teams are called out.

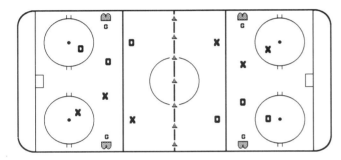

F 19

(1) Three-on-three with one puck.

(2) *Push puck scrimmage*: Players push the puck with gloves instead of using sticks.

(3) *Kick puck scrimmage*: Players use feet instead of sticks for scrimmage.

(4) *Backward skating only*: Players can only skate backwards while trying to score on the opposing team.

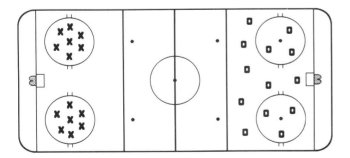

F 20

Demo derby: Players skate backward inside the circle and "bump" with their rear to knock players down. If they fall down for any reason, they are out of the circle.

Tag Games:

(1) *Back tag*: Everybody is "it." Tagged players go down on one knee and freeze.

(2) Coaches are "it."

(3) Choose two players to be "it."

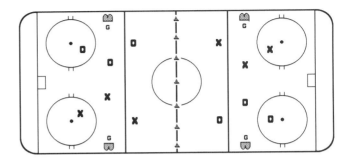

F 21

(1) *Fall down rule*: The coach blows the whistle during scrimmage, at which time all the players must fall down and get up as quickly as they can. The scrimmage continues.

(2) *Tight turn scrimmage*: The coach blows the whistle during scrimmage, at which time all the players must do a tight turn. The coach can designate if the players do a 180- or 360-degree tight turn, or if they go clockwise or counter-clockwise.

(3) *Checking scrimmage*: One team has its sticks upside-down. Change roles halfway through scrimmage.

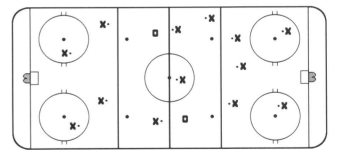

F 22

All the players (X) have pucks except two chasers (O). The players try to avoid the chasers, who attempt to steal the pucks. Once a chaser steals a puck from an X, the chaser puts the puck in the net and that particular player (X) now becomes a chaser (O). The drill is over when there is only one player left with a puck.

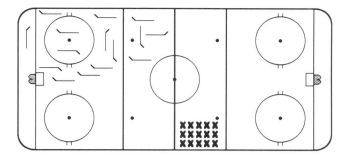

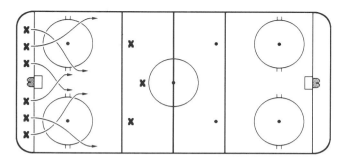

F 23

The players meet at the center red line on the boards and face the stands. The coaches then scatter the players' sticks around the ice in the end zone. Whoever finds his stick first and skates back to the start point is the winner.

F 26

All the players are behind the goal line except for three chasers who are in the neutral zone. The players try to get to the other goal line without being tagged by the chasers. Once tagged, the player is out. No sticks are used in this drill.

Variation: Once tagged, the player becomes a chaser.

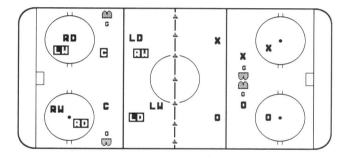

F 24

(1) *Five-on-five*: Wingers are in the offensive half of the ice only and defensive players are only in the defensive half of the ice. The centers can skate the entire zone.

(2) *Nets back-to-back*: Players try to win the scrimmage but the nets are back-to-back.

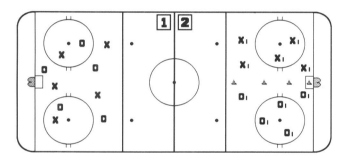

F 27

(1) *Team keep away*: Team X keeps the puck away from team O.

(2) *Puck battle*: Team X1 and team O1 shoot all the pucks they can to the other team's side. No one can cross the center. Coaches count the pucks after one minute to determine the winner.

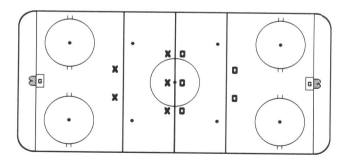

F 25

The team is divided in two for scrimmage five-on-five and the players play with a stick opposite to the way they shoot (i.e., right shots use left sticks and left shots use right sticks).

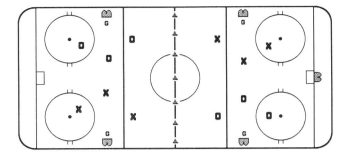

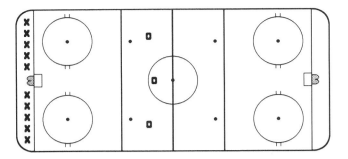

F 28

(1) *Score on either goalie*: Scrimmage as usual except players can score on either goalie. Keep score – it will be a challenge!

(2) *Three pass rule*: After every third pass in the scrimmage, the player must take a shot on goal.

F 31

Six cops and 10 to 15 robbers: The cops chase a robber, catch him (touch him), and put the robber in jail (center-ice circle). Rotate new cops in from time to time and allow for a jail break every once in a while.

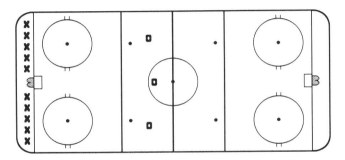

F 29

British Bulldog: All players line up on the goal line except three chasers who are in the neutral zone. The players try to skate to the far end of the ice without being touched by the chasers. Players caught by chasers become chasers for the next rush down the ice. The last player caught is the winner. In this version, players carry their sticks.

   Variation: Add pucks with chasers trying to knock puck off sticks.

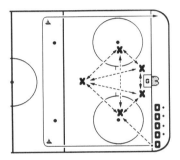

F 32

Baseball: First O passes the puck (flips it if more skilled) in front of goal. O then starts skating around the pylons for home base in the opposite corner. This would be a home run. While O is skating, X players must make five passes and after the fifth, that player must take a shot on goal. All X players must touch the puck once and only once before the shot can be taken. X players can move around the area. If an X player scores before O gets home, then O is out. If X players don't score before O gets home, the run counts. Three out to a side.

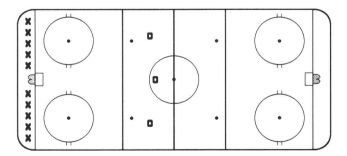

F 30

This game is the same as British Bulldog except the players hit the others with a ball. A maximum of six balls can be used. Use soft, all-purpose gym balls.

Bibliography

Advanced II Proceedings. Ottawa: Canadian Amateur Hockey Association, 1989.

Almstead, J. (Ed.) *On the Attack: A Drill Manual*. Ottawa: Canadian Amateur Hockey Association, 1990.

Bompa, T. *Theory and Methodology of Training*. Dubuque: Kendall/Hunt Pub. Co., 1985.

Canada Cup Observation Project. Ottawa: Canadian Amateur Hockey Association, 1981.

Coach Level Manual. Ottawa: Canadian Amateur Hockey Association, 1989.

Hockey Coaching Journal. Toronto: Hockey Coaching Journal Pub. Co., Vols. 1-5, 1989-1993.

Intermediate Level Manual. Ottawa: Canadian Amateur Hockey Association, 1989.

International Hockey Coaches Conference. Calgary, Ottawa: Canadian Amateur Hockey Association, 1989.

Kostka, V. *Czechoslovakian Youth Ice Hockey Training System*. Ottawa: Canadian Amateur Hockey Association, 1979.

Lener, Slavomir. *Transition Defense to Offense*. Ottawa: Canadian Amateur Hockey Association.

National Coaches Certification Program Level 1 Theory, Level 2 Theory, Level 3 Theory. Ottawa: Coaching Association of Canada, 1989.

Proceedings of NCCP Level V Seminar. Ottawa: Canadian Amateur Hockey Association, 1973, 1975, 1977, 1978, 1979, 1981, 1983, 1985.

Ogrean, D. and L. Vairo. *U.S.A. Hockey Coaches Drill Book*. Colorado Springs: Hockey U.S.A., 1979.

Palmer, G. *The Hockey Drill Book*. Champaign: Human Kinetics Publishing, 1984.

Proceedings of Elite Hockey Coaches Symposium. Toronto: York University, 1985, 1986, 1987, 1988.

Proceedings of Roger Neilson's Coaches' Clinic. Windsor, 1990, 1991, 1992, 1993.

Smith, R. *Hockey Practice Drills*. Toronto: Hockey Development Center of Ontario, 1982.